Post-Marxist Theory

THE SUNY SERIES IN
.POSTMODERN CULTURE
Joseph Natoli, *Editor*

Post-Marxist Theory

An Introduction

Philip Goldstein

State University of New York Press

Published by
State University of New York Press, Albany

For information, address State University of New York Press,
90 State Street, Suite 700, Albany, NY 12207

Production by Kelli Williams
Marketing by Anne M. Valentine

Library of Congress Cataloging-in-Publication Data
Goldstein, Philip.
    Post-Marxist theory : an introduction / Philip Goldstein.
        p. cm. — (SUNY series in postmodern culture)
    ISBN 0-7914-6301-X (alk. paper) — ISBN 0-7914-6302-8 (pbk. : alk.
paper)
        1. Communism.   2. Philosophy, Marxist.   3. Marxian economics.
I. Title.   II. Series.

HX73G62 2004
335.4—dc22   2004042983

Contents

Acknowledgments

I am grateful to Joseph Natoli, without whose encouragement I may not have put this book together. I am also grateful to the University of Delaware for the leave and the University of California at Berkeley for the facilities that enabled me to write this book. I thank my charming wife Leslie for her close, skeptical questioning of my views, my friends at the Marxist Literary Group for the many chances to present and discuss my work, and the readers and editors of *Rethinking Marxism*, published by the Taylor and Francis Group (http://www.tandf.co.uk/journals/titles/08935696.html) for their helpful comments and responses to my work. Portions of chapter 1 were originally published as "Communism and Postmodern Theory: A Revaluation of Althusser's Marxism," Rethinking Marxism, *Rethinking Marxism* 10:3 (Fall 1997), and portions of chapter five were originally published as "Between Althusserian Science and Foucauldian Materialism: The Later Work of Pierre Macherey," *Rethinking Marxism* 16:3 (July 2004). Chapter 6 includes highly revised portions of chapter 1 of my *Communities of Value* (Lexington Press, 2001). An early version of chapter 3 appeared as "Ernesto Laclau and Chantal Mouffe," in *Postmodernism: The Key Figures* (Blackwell Publishing, 2002).

When Gayatri Spivak's highly intellectual mother read her daughter's translation of Mr. Derrida . . . , she said, "But dear, how are you going to reconcile your communism with this?"

—Interview with Gayatri Spivak, *New York Times*
February 9, 2002

Introduction

From Marx to Post-Marxism

In 1973 Alice Walker flew to Eatonville, Florida, to plant a tombstone on Zora Neale Hurston's unmarked grave. Posing as Hurston's niece, she interviewed the physician, undertaker, and neighbors of Hurston and sought but did not find the grave in the cemetery's waist-high grass. Afterward, she commissioned a tombstone that declared Zora Neale Hurston "a genius of the South novelist folklorist anthropologist 1901 1960" ("Looking for Zora" 116). Walker says, "We are a people. A people do not throw their geniuses away" ("Tale" 69); however, after World War II the work of Hurston, the most prolific African American woman writer at that time, was neglected, and Hurston herself forced to accept employment as a maid and welfare support from the state. Moreover, to explain her ensuing oblivion, many critics fault the Marxist realists who, like Richard Wright and Ralph Ellison, considered Hurston a "good darkie" indifferent to social injustice and class conflict. As Mary Helen Washington says, "By the end of the forties, a decade dominated by Wright and the stormy fiction of social realism, the quieter voice of a woman searching for self-realization could not, or would not, be heard" (viii).[1]

As this critique of Richard Wright and the realists suggests, black feminism, which Walker, Toni Morrison, and

1

others initiated, faults the class analyses of traditional
Marxism because they emphasize the production of goods,
not the reproduction of the family, and the common class oppression of blacks, whites, women, or other peoples of color,
not their historically unique experiences. Such faults pose
what Angela Davis terms "the difficult question, yet unre-
solved in practice, of the relation between racism and national oppression on the one hand and exploitation at the
point of production on the other" (147).

    As I will show, what best explains the "relation between
racism and national oppression on the one hand and exploitation . . . on the other" is poststructuralist Marxism or
post-Marxism, a theory that I derive from the work of Louis
Althusser and Michel Foucault and which, thanks to their
extraordinary influence, has acquired philosophical, economic, historical, feminist, literary, and cultural versions.
Including Judith Butler, John Frow, Richard Wolf, Ernesto
Laclau, Tony Bennett, and others, the complex thinkers who
represent post-Marxism address many traditions and methods and do not form a movement or a school; however, they
all restate and revise Althusserian and/or Foucauldian theory, and, unlike traditional Marxism, which in Wright's fashion emphasizes the priority of class struggle and the
common humanity of oppressed groups, these scholars all reveal social life's sexual, racial, class, and ethnic divisions and
progressive import.

    Initiating post-Marxism, Althusser's account of Marx
undermines the humanist and the totalitarian views of
Marxism and opens the many schools and movements in
philosophy to such political critique. As chapter 1 indicates,
in the early work, he argues that, far from a reductive determinism, Marx's "theoretical practice" implicitly defines science in a formal way: it can grasp reality only if it
independently develops its concepts, not if it conforms with
practice, fact, or truth (*Marx* 182–93). By contrast, ideology,
an unsystematic, decentered network of socially necessary
images, myths, structures, and concepts, explains the subject's role in a society's socioeconomic structure, what Althusser calls the subject's relation to the relations of

production. Ideology, not theory, imposes the traditional "dialectical unity" of principles ("theory") and practice or ideas and facts.

In later work, Althusser rejects such theoretical autonomy, which he terms "theoreticism"; as he says, Marx repudiated "every philosophical ideology of the subject" because it "gave classical bourgeois philosophy the means of *guaranteeing* its ideas, practices, and goals" (*Essays* 178). As a result, he criticizes the broad opposition of science and ideology and in a Foucauldian manner examines a discourse or discipline's historical context of conventions and practices, what he calls its "problematic." He still maintains that a particular science or discourse resists the ideological commitments that form part of its history; however, he claims that, in keeping with the conventions, norms, and ideals that make up its context or "problematic," each science elaborates its own theoretical concepts. Economics, history, philosophy, mathematics, and other scientific disciplines and practices do not develop a general opposition of ideology and science; in accord with their distinct problematics, they establish their own "inward" criteria of validity and produce their own legitimate objects and discourses.

He argues that, because diverse discourses evolve different versions of the science/ideology, the many schools and movements in philosophy are open to political critique, what he calls class struggle in theory. Despite this post-Marxist turn, he never abandoned the traditional notion of economic determination in that last instance or the traditional faith in the working class and its political parties. As he affirms in his popular autobiography, "[N]o other organization in France, I say really no other organization in France, can offer sincere militants a formation and practical political experience comparable to those that one can acquire in the [French communist] party" (*L'avenir* 226; my translation).

Michel Foucault says that the study of the Soviet Gulag exposes the limits of the party as well as Marxism (Foucault, *Power/Knowledge* 134–37). He discusses the breakdown of the phenomenological tradition, not Marxism's humanist or Stalinist limitations. He examines discourse, not the opposition of science and ideology, because he considers science "one practice among many." He claims that the changing institutional contexts and the ruptures or gaps in a discourse's historical development, not the autonomous norms nor the objective truths of a scientific theory, explain the history of a discourse and open it to critique. It is, nonetheless, true that, like Althusser, who was his teacher and colleague, Foucault dismisses humanist and scientific notions of theoretical self-consciousness and distinguishes the discourses of power/knowledge from the ruling class' unifying interests.

In his early works, he emphasizes the Nietzschean notion that discourse does not uncover a preexistent object; discourse constitutes the objects, including the human "object," which it purports to uncover. In his later works, he examines the sociopolitical import of distinct discourses, whose power to constitute a subject extends not only to the individual but also to the "social" subject. As a consequence, while Althusser preserves traditional notions of economic determination and working-class or communist party politics, Foucault's positive, factual genealogies of punishment or sexuality implicitly foster the politics of marginal groups, what Ernesto Laclau and Chantal Mouffe term a radical coalition of women's, black, and other "new social movements."

Laclau and Mouffe defend these movements. They also adopt the Althusserian theory that the ideological apparatuses of the state interpellate or construct a subject and, thereby, reproduce themselves, rather than the Hegelian belief that predetermined historical stages and contexts explain social development. Where they differ is that in a poststructuralist fashion they develop Gramsci's notion of ideological hegemony. As I show in chapter 3, they maintain that, since objects do not simply or literally mirror their sociohistorical contexts, the distinction between object and context, discursive and nondiscursive practices, or "thought and reality" breaks down; in Laclau and Mouffe's terms, "[s]ynonomy, metonomy, metaphor . . . are part of the primary terrain itself in which the social is constituted" (*Hegemony*, 110).

In the 1970s and 1980s, the Soviet Union is close to its demise, the Western working class has turned conservative, and independent movements of women, blacks, homosexuals, and others have developed. In this context Laclau and Mouffe suggest that, while hegemonic ideologies constitute the conservative identities of the working class, women, minorities, and others, their hostilities or "antagonisms," not socioeconomic contradictions, expose the fissures within these identities. In other words, while the interests of trade unions and management objectively oppose each other, they may work together harmoniously, whereas women, Hispanics, blacks, or Asians may angrily oppose unfair or discriminatory state or industrial policies even though the objective interests of those groups are not contradictory.

Laclau and Mouffe claim, as a consequence, that the discursive conflicts by which contending political parties seek to impose their hegemony explain values and identities more fully than ruling-class interests or social structures do because, incomplete or dislocated, such structures produce only partial identities. The subject remains fissured because the antagonisms of diverse social movements or the dislocation of social structures matters more than the systematic contradictions and predetermined structures of the traditional view (*Hegemony* 122–34). Laclau forcefully demonstrates, moreover, that a successful politics requires strategic argument whose success predetermined working-class or other socioeconomic contexts cannot ensure in advance. Opening discourse to the theoretical critique rejected by Foucault and, to an extent, Althusser, he maintains that, while the black, feminist, gay, and ethnic social movements properly defend their separate interests or their political independence, each movement must construct equivalent ideals establishing a new hegemonic bloc because what establishes identity is contextual oppositions, antagonisms, or exclusions, not essences or transcendent selves.

Well known as a feminist, Hegelian, and queer theorist, Judith Butler also adopts the poststructuralist or post-Marxist theories of Althusser, Foucault, and Laclau and Mouffe. As I indicate in chapter 4, she, like them, critiques the humanist assumption that the subject asserts its individual or prediscursive autonomy and agency and adopts the post-structuralist belief that ideology interpellates or discourses of power/knowledge discipline the subject. They maintain, however, that science preserves its independence of ideology or that hegemonic ideologies constitute fissured subjects, whereas she says that the heterosexual norms imposed by power govern the construction of gender. While traditional feminists assume that the terms "male" and "female" identify biologically distinct groups with equally distinct interests, experiences, and social organizations, she takes Althusser's and Foucault's views to suggest that gender is not a matter of human nature or biological traits but a performance imposed by established cultural norms.

Like Laclau and Mouffe, she defends resistance or theoretical critique, but she assumes that the heterosexual norms imposed by institutional practices preclude the political liberation sought by oppositional theorists. In the early *Gender Trouble* she argues that, as parody or drag, sexuality still fosters resistance or makes gender trouble by multiplying or parodying the categories of gender (34). In later work, she goes on to adopt Freudian or Lacanian notions of the unconscious as well as post-Marxist versions of a radical democracy. While the Freudian notions contradict or, as she says, "supplement" the Foucauldian approach, making subjugation the desire of the complicitous subject, the post-Marxist account democratizes her notion of gender, opening it to articulation by African American, third world, and other peoples of color.

Pierre Macherey also adopts Althusserian Marxism and Foucauldian poststructuralism, but, unlike Butler and Laclau and Mouffe, he repudiates Freudian, Nietzschean, and Hegelian modes of theoretical critique and seeks significant historical depth. In his early work, which includes *A Theory of Literary Production* and *Hegel ou Spinoza* (1979), Macherey, who was Althusser's student, colleague, and collaborator for more than ten years, defends the Althusserian belief that scientific Marxism opposes Stalinist and humanist theory and that literature, situated between science and ideol-

ogy, shows but does not tell the truth. In his later work, including *A quoi pense la littérature?* (*What does literature
think about?* [1990]) and *Histoires de dinosaure* (*Histories of
a dinosaur* [1999]), Macherey repudiates his earlier scientific antihumanism and, inspired by Foucault, adopts a historical or "materialist" perspective in which, never pure,
independent, or scientific, theory is always situated in a
practical context in which it reveals the antagonisms of and
takes a position on the contrary views forming the context.
While Laclau and Mouffe and Butler admit the democratizing articulations or translations of the women's, black, postcolonial, or other new social movements, Macherey defends
a philosophical realism that denies the incommensurable,
"relativist" perspectives of such movements; nonetheless,
Macherey argues that the productive activities not only of
authors but of readers as well give a literary or a philosophical text its meaning and, despite or because of their errors,
their accounts explain its history.

The cultural theory of Tony Bennett, John Frow, and
Toby Miller also rejects the scientific theory of the Althusserian tradition and examines the interpretive activity or democratic articulations of diverse readers. In chapter 6, I show
that, like Pierre Macherey, Bennett and Frow initially elaborate scientific Althusserian theory, which construes literary
realism as the effect of established conventions, not the imitation of an independent reality, and literary texts as intertextual practices, not ideological forms. Bennett and Frow
also go on to show that the interpretive practices of readers,
rather than Althusserian science, explain a text's import and,
more generally, literature's history; however, like Laclau and
Mouffe and Butler, Frow defends the subversive force of critical theory, while, more radically than Macherey, Bennett,
and Miller deny the aesthetic norms of cultural practices
and emphasize the historical and institutional contexts of literary reception.

As the work of these scholars suggest, Althusser's antihumanist Marxism and Foucault's genealogical studies have
initiated a post-Marxism that rejects "objective" humanist
guarantees of transcendent reality and public life and

reveals the constitutive or hegemonic import of discourse. In *Marx@2000*, Ronaldo Munck rightly says that, thanks to these late or post-Marxist theorists, "[w]e are now much more aware of the diversity of capitalism and the plurality of social struggles. Race, gender, sexuality, religion, disability, and region are all on this terrain, alongside and integrated with class" (73); however, he considers those who deny or reject the "plurality of social struggles" and defend the traditional notion of class context rigid fundamentalists who "retreat into blind dogmatism."[2] The post-Marxists do, for the most part, depict this "terrain," but the difficulties of traditional Marxism involve more than "blind dogmatism."

No one would call Fredric Jameson, for example, a blind dogmatist, yet he defends Marxism's traditional doctrines, including a "complex" distinction of base/superstructure, objective accounts of class contexts, systematic practices of revolutionary change, the global economy as late capitalism's totality, and the Frankfurt School's critique of commodity fetishism. One reason is that, since he considers Stalinism a positive modernizing force whose enviable successes gave it worldwide influence ("Existing" 43–4), he does not admit that the Soviet historical experience or conservative totalitarian theory raise significant epistemological issues or that post-Marxism differs from Eduard Bernstein's revisionist socialism ("Existing" 21). He also denies that the formal autonomy of the sciences or the disciplines or the independence of the women's, black, and ethnic movements raise significant issues; rather, in Georg Lukács's humanist fashion he complains that what he calls the "fragmentation and compartmentalization of social reality in modern times" (*Fables* 6) divides the surfaces of life from its depths, effaces its "underlying unity," and acquires an obsessive, dominating force. As he says, this unity "would remain merely symbolic, a mere methodological fiction, were it not understood that social life is in its fundamental reality one and indivisible, a seamless web, a single inconceivable and transindividual process" (*Political* 40). Michael Ryan rightly points out that "one effect" of Jameson's work on postmodernism "was to assure that . . . that the old models and languages of understanding within Marxism would stand, that the moral and intellectual order assured by the ascendancy of those languages and models would hold" (2). In general, because the communist countries turned into dictatorships and the academic or scientific disciplines and the modern social movements achieved independence, these "old models and languages of understanding," including the humanist ideals and historical methodology of Karl Marx, present epistemological difficulties which post-Marxism addresses but traditional Marxism and its contemporary defenders, including Jameson, ignore or dismiss.

The Difficulties of Traditional Marxism

These difficulties, especially the communist dictatorship and the disciplines' and movements' independence, arise because traditional Marxism defends Karl Marx's reductive belief that socioeconomic changes explain the historical evolution of capitalist society and justify a communist revolution that restores the human or social powers of society. Traditional Marxism takes Marx to show that philosophy, theology, economics, or art do not have a history apart from that of their socioeconomic systems; rather, the theoretical activity of the ruling class and its representatives brings these discourses together to form a unity ("form of consciousness") that expresses and justifies the social system. As Marx says in *The German Ideology*,

> Morality, religion, metaphysics, all the rest of ideology and their corresponding forms of consciousness, thus no longer retain the semblance of independence. They have no history, no development; but men . . . alter, along with . . . their real existence, their thinking and the products of their thinking. (14)

Old and Young Hegelians alike believe that the mind or spirit ("forms of consciousness") is self-determining or self-constituting, but Marx rejects this belief: "In direct contrast to German philosophy which descends from heaven to earth, we ascend from earth to heaven" (47). To an extent, this claim simply denies that the "forms of consciousness" determine themselves. The mind of the intellectual does not control or change historical circumstances; rather, these circumstances influence the development of consciousness and its forms because "men . . . alter, along with . . . their real existence, their thinking and the products of their thinking."

At the same, Marx faults the fetishized character of ideas and goods. In the case of ideas, Marx maintains that the ruling elites may present them as universal, but in a particular society certain ideas prevail because they and not other ideas best defend the interests of the ruling elites; in his terms, "[t]he ideas of the ruling class are in every epoch the ruling ideas" (64). The figure of the ruling class stresses the interested character of "ideas," what Gramsci calls their hegemonic force (52–5).

Moreover, drawing on classical economics, which claims that labor creates the values embedded in commodities, Marx argues that the division of labor alienates the working class from its products, including the products of thought.[3] Although the labor of the working class gives commodities their value, capitalist production embues them with the mystical powers that tribal societies reserve for their totemic gods. Instead of using commodities, people worship them. People have diverse ends and purposes, but commodity production destroys the ability of individuals to define themselves; their products—cars, machines, theories—impose definition, self, and purpose upon them. Such "fetishized" commodities displace and conceal the social relations organizing society and acquire the rationality and the value lost to humanity (Marx, *Capital* 69–84; Fromm, *Man*; Jameson, *Form* 232–57).

In the critical, Hegelian manner, Marx argues that communists take action to overcome the fetishized production of goods and ideas by ending the division of labor grounding it. In other words, since the working class produces the values that commodities embody and the ruling class appropriates and divides up the resulting surplus value, commodities acquire a reified character, but the communist revolution, which abolishes the division of labor, overcomes the reified character of wealth and reinstates the working class' unalienated, human self. As he says, "*All-round* dependence . . . will be transformed by this communist revolution into the control and conscious mastery of these powers, which, born of the action of men on one another, have till now overawed and governed men as powers completely alien to them" (*German* 55).

Marx claims, in other words, not only that the historical evolution of a capitalist society explains the development of its philosophical systems or artistic forms but also that a communist revolution overcomes the fetishism of commodities and restores the human or social powers of a society. Many scholars object, however, that in this account "ideas" come to mirror socioeconomic history passively, losing any vestige of autonomous development (See David Caute 153–57; Terry Eagleton, *Marxism* 34; Frederic Jameson, *Prison-House* 213–14; Alan Swingewood 21; and Raymond Williams, *Marxism* 59). They claim that Marx's belief that sociohistorical circumstances govern the evolution of consciousness amounts to a reductive form of socioeconomic determinism and even a justification of totalitarian communism.

This difficulty with Marx's view stems from two distinct twentieth-century developments: the growth and collapse of Soviet communism, which produced the Stalinist dictatorship, and the independence of modern disciplines and social movements, which undermine the humanist ideal of the unified, autonomous self. Consider, to begin with, the difficulties represented by Soviet communism. In the very influential *Totalitarian Dictatorship and Autocracy* (1956), Zbiginew Brzezinski and Carl J. Friedrich say that the rational ideals that Marx acquired from the French Enlightenment provided communism's key ideas, such as "total democracy," "rationalistic" revolution, and absolute political unanimity (82–83). As I explain more fully in chapter 3, these empirical political scientists claim that those ideas

account for communism's totalitarian characteristics—a
dogmatic ideology sanctioned by the state, a monolithic
party ruled by a dictator, a terroristic system of police control, and a monopoly of communications, arms and weapons,
and economic production (56).

Like Theodor Adorno and other Frankfurt School theorists, Herbert Marcuse sharply condemns the "reified" empirical outlook of Brzezinski, Friedrich, and the political
scientists, but he too derives totalitarian communism from
the Western Enlightenment. He too argues that the scientific rationality imposed by the Enlightenment explains the
repressive practices of the former Soviet state. In *One-
Dimensional Man*, for example, Marcuse admits that the totalitarian dictatorship of the Soviet Communist Party
intends to produce enlightenment and independence; however, just as Brzezinski and Friedrich claim that Western
technology explains totalitarian practices, so Marcuse argues that Soviet Marxism perpetuates what he calls "technical progress as the instrument of domination" (41–42).
Brzezinksi and Friedrich say that the blind, fanatic ideology
of the Soviet Communist Party precludes rational thought;
similarly, Marcuse claims that the technological rationality
dominating the former USSR successfully stifled critical
thought and absorbed the working class and other, oppositional groups.

Lastly, in *The Master Thinkers*, the conservative André
Glucksman admits that, rejecting Hegelian dialectics, Marx
substitutes the class or the party for the Hegelian "I" or the
Fichtean "ego"; Glucksman claims, however, that Marx still
seeks the idealist mastery or, in Hegelian terms, the "dialectical unity" in which the self or the party are self-sufficient
(204). Glucksman also admits that Marx critiques the development of capital, not of the Spirit, but concludes that, even
though Marx seeks to end capitalist power over social institutions, his Hegelian theory effectively hands them over to
the communist bureaucrats building their private dachas
and organizing their torturous gulags (226).

In other words, empirical political scientists and conservative and radical scholars all maintain that Marx's the-

ory explains the communist totalitarian nightmare. In addition, the difficulties of Marx's view stem from the independence of modern disciplines and social movements, which undermine the humanist ideals of the unified, autonomous self. Before I discuss these difficulties, I should note that some contemporary scholars dismiss them on the textual grounds that Marx's work resists the methodological dogmas fostered by Engels, Marx's first editor; his later Soviet editors; as well as Lenin, Stalin, and numerous others.[4] For example, Richard Marsden says that, first published in 1934, *The German Ideology* does not formulate the materialist conception of history, as traditional Marxists claim. Their claim depends upon the first chapter, which, "formed by gathering together the various rough-drafted and scattered theoretical sections of the manuscript," was created by the Soviet editors, who were the first to publish the book (72–73). Setting the chapter in the context of Marx's political activity and evolving thought, Marsden argues that, like Marx's other early works, the chapter describes the relationship of the "atomic" citizen or civil society and the political state, not the influence of the base on the superstructure. This mainly biographical account of *The German Ideology* assumes, however, that the critical mind of the genius shines above the movements and schools that establish and dispute his import. Marsden says that we value traditional Marxism because "[i]t has a familiar, necessary quality. We are grateful to it, for it was better than the alternatives, and better than nothing at all" (45); actually, it matters because, even though it may not get Marx's views right, it made his work important.

Traditional Marxism claims, in particular, that Marx's theory represents the humanist ideal of critical thought rejected not only by scientific Stalinists and totalitarian theorists but also poststructuralists such as Lyotard or Foucault. For example, Raymond Williams, who was a communist militant in his youth, disavowed traditional Marxism because of its reductive passivity (*Culture and Society* 209–84). In the 1960s, when he returned to Marxism, he adopted a Hegelian view, which claims that great thinkers or artists articulate what he calls the "structure of feeling" of those who share the thinker's milieu, class, or experience and which preserves the traditional Marxist notion that historical development explains the evolution of ideas. This Hegelian view effectively overcomes this passivity, resisting both the established doctrines of scientific Marxism and the abstract jargon of postmodern theory (*Problems* 18–22). Similarly, Christopher Hill, E. P. Thompson, Arnold Kettle, Alvin Kiernan, and other British critics and scholars supported the British Communist Party in the 1940s and 1950s, but represented a humanist opposition to scientific Stalinism. In the 1960s and 1970s they adopted independent leftist stances and, in the 1970s and 1980s, went on to oppose structuralist and poststructuralist Marxism, which Thompson derisively labeled the "poverty of theory."[5]

Marx and traditional Marxists consider humanism a universal truth transcending and opposing contemporary movements or fashions; however, the modern humanist ideal of a unified or autonomous self begins in the eighteenth-century Enlightenment, when Kant argued that the subjective categories of human reason and the categorical imperatives of the human will dominate nature (see Davies 117–24), and breaks down in the twentieth century, when scientific or academic disciplines acquire formal autonomy. As Foucault says in *Les Mots et Les Choses*, the figure of man

> is a quite recent creature, which the demiurge of knowledge fabricated with its own hands less than two hundred years ago: but he has grown old so quickly that it has been only too easy to imagine that he had been waiting for thousands of years in the darkness for that moment of illumination in which he would be finally known ("Avant la fin du xviiie siècle, l'*homme* n'existait pas. . . . C'est une toute rècent crèature que la dèmiurge du savoir a fabriquée de ses mains, il y a moins de deux cents ans: mais il a si vite vieilli, qu'on a imaginé facilement qu'il avait attendu dans l'ombre pendant des millénaires le moment d'illumination où il serait enfin connu"). (308)

The nineteenth century invented what Tony Davies calls "the myth of essential and universal Man: essential, because humanity . . . is the inseparable and central essence . . . of human beings; universal, because that essential humanity is shared by all human beings, of whatever time or place" (24). Applied to the working-class movement, this myth explains Marx's belief that wage-labor alienates the worker from what Feuerbach termed his or her species-essence. Applied to literary study, the myth formed what Matthew Arnold called "disinterested" humanism, which, by appealing to the reader's "best" self, would reconcile the social classes and unify the state.

Moreover, this modern humanism differs substantially from Renaissance humanism. A loose collection of peregrinating scholars whose friendships concealed their many differences, the Renaissance humanists esteemed classical eloquence as well as the ancient Greeks and Romans but never formed a coherent movement or overcame chauvinist sentiments and adopted truly universal human ideals (see Davies 72–104). Early Renaissance humanists, including Rudolph Agricola and Desiderius Erasmus, claimed that the study of classical rhetoric would ensure that the good speaker is a good man. These humanists argued that, unlike the dry scholastic logic of the medieval era, classical rhetoric fostered the religious, moral, and civic virtue of the good orator. Ensconced in the endowed private schools and great universities, this Latinate humanist theory justified the aristocracy, the clergy, and the Tudor court, whose vast patronage made it a central route to wealth and power, not the grounds of social criticism (see Altick 173–87; and Frank Whigham).

Later humanists also believed that good rhetoric promotes virtue, decorum, or civility; however, inspired by Ramus, these humanists treated rhetorical techniques as useful skills applicable to law, government, and other areas (see Walter J. Ong 6; Thomas M. Conley 109–10; and Anthony Grafton and Lisa Jardine 161–200). More importantly, the later humanists justified the use of the "vulgar" vernacular languages, rather than the learned Latin. Successful in the marketplace, the church, dissenting adult schools, commercial academies, female seminaries, but not in the university, the later humanist defense of a vernacular rhetoric promoted the English language and literature of the nationalist middle class. Codifying the practices of Renaissance humanism, this neoclassical humanist criticism flourished in the eighteenth century, when it was able to unite the aristocracy and the middle classes, and to define the educated public or, as Jürgen Habermas says, the public sphere (See Eric Auerbach 333; Gerald Newman 67–87; Patrick Parringer 8; and René Wellek I: 5–11); however, in the nineteenth century, when the middle classes acquired more power, partisan journals formed diverse publics, and the modern disciplines acquired formal autonomy, the neoclassical ideal lost its ability to unite the aristocracy and the bourgeoisie.[6]

Foucault and François Lyotard both show that this breakdown of humanism enables the disciplines to acquire a formal autonomy contrary to humanist ideals. As I indicate in chapter 3, Foucault says that, to ground the disciplines, the nineteenth-century episteme invents the figure of man, whom the eighteenth century does not discuss; in the twentieth century, however, the modern episteme, which breaks into the mathematical sciences, the social sciences, and philosophical disciplines, subverts the human figure grounding the disciplines and allows them to establish their formal autonomy. Similarly, in *The Postmodern Condition* Lyotard says that in the twentieth century, the traditional grand narratives, which include Marxist accounts of historical development, Christian accounts of religious salvation, and liberal accounts of social progress, can no longer justify the specialized sciences or disciplines, which, as a result, provide their own legitimating "ideological" rationales (60).

Georg Lukács, the most important traditional Marxist, defends the autonomy and rationality of the humanist subject and the revolutionary potential of the working class and opposes the reified character of commodity production, the breakdown of the public sphere, and the divisions and independence of the disciplines and social movements. In the early *The Theory of the Novel*, he accepts the Kantian belief that ethical or aesthetic norms preserve freedom and autonomy (65) but argues that, contrary to Kant, who maintained that we cannot know the thing-in-itself, experience reveals real essences or underlying conditions (48–55). He also adopts the historical method of G. W. F. Hegel, who argues in *The Phenomenology of Mind* that outside of consciousness or "appearance" the Kantian essence or thing-in-itself reduces to an empty abstraction, a substanceless ideal.

Lukács preserves and extends Hegel's systematizing account of experience but repudiates Hegel's faith in absolute knowledge because Lukács fears that, in pursuing such an absolute consciousness, the philosopher experiences an alienating and vitiating self-consciousness. The young Lukács construes this self-consciousness as a legitimate mode of historical understanding and critique. In the later *History and Class Consciousness*, Lukács condemns this Hegelian self-consciousness as kind of disorientation and isolation. To overcome it, he turns to Marx and Feuerbach, who suggest that the limited totalities of "practical" men relieve this self-consciousness and justify political action. Revising and extending Marx's critique of commodity production, Lukács argues that capitalism extends the commodity's illusory autonomy to all social institutions (83–110).

More precisely, he divorces commodity production from the labor theory of value which Marx derives from classical economics and which justifies Marx's critique of commodity fetishism. Marxist economists defend a revised labor theory of value against modern economics, which has rejected that theory; by contrast, Lukács, who denies the autonomy of the disciplines, treats commodity fetishism as objectively valid. He claims that it grounds an instrumental rationality, which calculates means and not ends, evaluates techniques and not values, and seeks autonomy and not community. As J. M. Bernstein points out, Lukács maintains that, once economic institutions gain their independence, capitalism imposes this rationality on all realms, including the intellectual (82). The sciences, the humanities, and the other disciplines functioning within this context examine the internal relations of their disciplines and ignore their social relations. Like commodities, these "reified" disciplines consider themselves autonomous and ignore their underlying social conditions.

In *The Dialectic of Enlightenment*, Theodor Adorno and Max Horkheimer also assume that, divorced from the labor theory of value, a general instrumental rationality governs bourgeois social institutions, including the disciplines. Adorno and Horkheimer too claim that the sophisticated dialectics of Hegelian theory overcome these reified institutions and reveal the critical insights of great art or theory; however, more negative than Lukács, who defends the working class' revolutionary potential, they argue that, while empirical science sought to dismiss primitive mythology and superstition and to control nature, science produced, instead, its own mythology. Unlike the great art work, which retains the absolute totality and spiritual aura of the old, primitive myth, this scientific mythology denigrated nature, reified logic, aesthetics, information, and the status quo, and ensured, thereby, the conformity and the repression of the masses, including the working class.[7] In other words, the Enlightenment itself, not just Marxism, is "totalitarian" (6).

In the early work, Lukács also expects the lost totalities of the great art work to provide independent grounds of social critique, but in the influential essay "Reification and the Consciousness of the Proletariot" Lukács argues that history does not provide a perspective critical enough to demolish the reified state of modern society. The autonomous ethical subject of the modern era can oppose but cannot destroy society's reified forms of commodity production. In addition, the critic must adopt the terrain of the working class, the only class whose practical activity can overcome the divisions and the conflicts of social life. With fascism recently defeated, the cold war underway, and the capitalist economy booming, Marcuse, Adorno, and Horkheimer argue that instrumental rationality assimilates the working class, whereas, in 1921, when the Soviet revolution was still flowering and even Western revolutions looked possible, an optimistic Lukács moves to the USSR because he believes that the working class is "the identical subject-object of the social and historical processes of evolution" (149).

Jürgen Habermas also denies that the working class possesses this revolutionary import or that the "forms of consciousness" or instrumental reason imposes ruling-class domination. In *The Philosophical Discourse of Modernity*, he grants that the lifeworld or historical context explains the evolution of an era's ideas or the presuppositions of a writer or speaker and that the "system" of social institutions rationalizes and distorts the lifeworld, as Marx said. Habermas argues, just the same, that, far from totalitarian, the institutional "rationalization" produced by Enlightenment reason overcomes the reified character of the social system and, as the neoclassical humanists said, maintains the independent public spheres of art, ethics, and science (112–19). He says that rational communication mitigates the reified character of economics, the law, or disciplinary knowledge and fosters the democratic practices instituted by the Enlightenment. What determines the best argument is the rules governing validity claims in each public sphere, not the social status or economic influence possessed by the speaker. As a result, the best argument will prevail provided those who engage in debate in the public spheres set aside their partisan interests and seek consensus. Moreover, more than the effaced totality of the working class revolution, the modern university which, by making technical or specialized knowledge accessible to the uninitiated, overcomes the reified disciplines and preserves the public spheres.

In this way Habermas's account of Enlightenment reason justifies the specialized, disciplinary knowledge repudiated by the traditional Hegelian humanism of Lukács and Adorno and Horkheimer; still, while he also faults the subjectivity of Kantian humanism as well as its division between pure and practical reason, he preserves its autonomous norms (see Strong and Sposito 268–81). For example, he maintains that what explains totalitarian oppression is not Enlightenment rationality but its breakdown, what he terms the failure of "praxis philosophy" to clarify its "normative foundations" or to oppose the communists' false totalities (*Modernity* 66–8; see also John Brenkman 83–5 and 104–106). This account accommodates the conservative, totalitarian account of communism but on the basis of a Kantian "self-reflection." That is, the totalitarian theorists say that Marx shared the Enlightenment's overly optimistic view of science and technology; Habermas fears that Marx remains too committed to the Fichtean "ego" of the industrial engineer to provide for that moment of self-reflection in which the theorist explains and critiques the intellectual contexts influencing social thought (*Knowledge* 46–8).

His critique of postmodern theory also reveals a Kantian bias. He complains that, "young conservatives," the postmodernists forcefully reject the theoretical totalizing whereby Hegel resists the philosophical context of the modern subject, but they do not escape the limits of the modern subject or establish the validity of their theoretical ideals. He fears, moreover, that their critique of Enlightenment reason discourages rational communication and destroys the liberal consensus legitimating art, ethics, science, and other public spheres. These critiques of postmodernism as well as his account of communicative action preserve the Kantian ideals of rational truth, individual autonomy, and common sense. As I will show in chapter 3, Ernesto Laclau and Chantal Mouffe's post-Marxist notion of ideological hegemony acknowledges the socioeconomic inequity and ruling-class domination of social life and fosters a democratic alliance of the women's, black, and ethnic movements; by contrast, his forceful critique of Lukácsian humanism grants the independence of the disciplines and their public spheres, but his defense of communicative reason preserves humanist notions of rational equality and denies the independence of the modern social movements.[8]

Conclusion

In general, traditional Marxism and its humanist defenders oppose specialized disciplinary discourse as well as structuralist and poststructuralist theory on the grounds that, more effectively than any theory, Marx's humanist ideals or socioeconomic theories overcome the divisions and fragmentation of modern social life and justify political critique, if not a communist revolution. As Randy Martin says,

> What compels acceptance of given marxist foundations is precisely that they do provide a way of lining up theoretical framework, historical project, and political organization. This alignment between Marx, socialism, and the left draws upon a powerful tradition and provides a comprehensive framework for action and reflection that has yet to be equaled. (xiv)

Such defenses of "Marxist foundations" accommodate the totalitarian critique of Marx or ignore or deny it as well as the independence of disciplinary knowledge and of modern social movements. In Martin's terms, "History has not erased Marx, but vindicated him"(xiv). Antihumanists such as Étienne Balibar and Alain Badiou also defend traditional Marxism, but, as I show in later chapters, their defenses face similar difficulties. By contrast, the post-Marxism initiated by Althusser's account of ideology and critique of humanist and Stalinist theory as well as Foucault's genealogies of discourse rejects "objective" humanist guarantees of rational truth, human independence, and public life and reveals the constitutive or hegemonic import of discourse. Some of these post-Marxists preserve the normative force of Freudian, Hegelian, or critical theory and justify thereby the radically democratic articulations, translations, or potential hegemony of oppositional or independent movements. Other post-Marxists emphasize the sociohistorical contexts of modern discursive practices, not the ideals of theoretical critique, and as a result open these practices to political critique. The work of all these scholars suggests, nonetheless, that, unlike traditional Marxism, which defends the priority of class struggle and the common humanity of oppressed groups, post-Marxism reveals the sexual, racial, class, and ethnic divisions of social life and promotes its progressive transformation.

Economics and Theory

Althusserian Post-Marxism

In the popular autobiography *The Future Lasts Forever*, Althusser says that, during the fatal weekend in which he murdered his wife Hélène Rytman, they argued very violently. On Sunday morning he awoke to find her lying dead, her neck broken, and he ran through the courtyard yelling "I've strangled Hélène." To explain why, he confesses that, born in Algeria, raised Catholic and celibate, and living in Paris, he studied philosophy, married Hélène, joined the Communist Party, and acquired high academic status. At the same time, he engaged in real and imagined sexual affairs with which he tormented Hélène and suffered from bleak depressions that often sent him to a mental hospital.

Before the murder his reputation and influence were waning, but after the murder his reputation suffered a serious decline. Several reviewers suggested that the scandalous murder, not the Marxist theory, sums up his work's meaning. In George Steiner's words, "what subsists" of Althusser's "influential" thought is "the piteous scandal of the life" (118). His work has, nonetheless, influenced many contemporary theorists, who include Tony Bennett, Judith Butler, John Frow, Michel Foucault, Ernesto Laclau, Pierre Macherey, Toby Miller, Chantal Mouffe, Stephen Resnick, and Richard Wolff.[1]

Despite the decline of his reputation and the "piteous scandal of the life," his work remains influential but in different ways. It is well known that in his structuralist phase Althusser defends the scientific character of Marxism and undermines the humanist import of the traditional and the Hegelian schools. The faults of his defense are also well known: as scholars have shown, Althusser's Marxism preserves the traditional belief that the economy determines social life, at least in the last instance, as well as the rationalist faith that the world conforms with the systematic mind (see Montag 72 and Hirst, *Law* 43–46). Less familiar, Althusser's critique of Marxism's foundational ideals has fostered poststructuralist or post-Marxist approaches which expose a discourse's figural or subjective import, including its racial, sexual, class, gendered, or political character.

The Structuralist Marxism of Louis Althusser

Althusser's structuralist approach first emerges in *For Marx*, which brings together his essays on the young Marx, dialectics, theater, science, and humanism. In the late 1950s and the early 1960s, when he wrote these essays, Marxism-Leninism, the French Communist Party, and the French Left enjoyed an unusual prestige. At the same time, the ongoing revelations of Stalinist dogma and brutality or totalitarian oppression led Marxists to revive the early, humanist works of Karl Marx.

Althusser grants that that Feuerbach's humanism influenced the young Marx, but he argues that Marx repudiated this speculative humanism and adopted a scientific outlook. A critic of established religion, Feuerbach argued that, by attributing society's powers to God, religion alienates human kind from its essential powers or "species-being." Even though a society's art, science, industry, government, or education produced impressive works, the established religion attributed these achievements to God's will, divine providence, or some equally mystical figure, not to humanity's social powers. A critic of Hegel, Feuerbach also argued that what Hegel calls the "cunning of reason" mystifies social forces in a similar way; they simply develop the predeter-

mined rationality of the world spirit, not the inherent poten-
tiality of their own powers.

Althusser admits that this secular, humanist critique of
religion and Hegel allowed Marx "to think" the contradiction
between the state's "essence (reason) and its existence (un-
reason)" (*Marx* 225). Still, Althusser insists that in *The German Ideology* Marx discovered the faults of Feuerbach's
theory: it remains speculative. Like Hegel, Feuerbach does
not abstract the theoretical concepts of the mind from the nature of empirical reality; he idly deduces empirical reality
from the mind's concepts and, denies, as a result, the authen-
ticating force of what Marx calls "sensuous human activity"
(*German* 197). Althusser suggests that, unlike Feuerbach,
Marx rejects Hegel's speculative self-consciousness and goes
on to develop a purely scientific Marxism; as Althusser says,
the "rupture with every *philosophical* anthropology or humanism is no secondary detail; it is Marx's scientific discovery" (*Marx* 227).

To justify this rupture with "all philosophical humanism," Althusser develops a rationalist view of science. He argues that it can grasp reality only if it rigorously develops its
concepts and its terms, not if it conforms with practice, fact,
or truth. In these formal terms, scientific theory establishes
its own criteria of truth; by contrast, what Althusser calls
ideology imposes the familiar conformity of theory and practice or ideas and facts. This conformity is not altogether negative. It is well known that Althusser endowed ideology with
a positive role: like the Foucauldian notion of discourse,
which I discuss in the next chapter, it constructs or "interpellates" a subject. Ideology does not represent falsehood or
misrepresentation; ideology explains the subject's role in a
society's socioeconomic structure, what Althusser calls the
subject's relation to the relations of production. Because theory preserves its own criteria of validity, he claimed,
nonetheless, that theory resists this ideological interpellation and effectively grasps the nature of reality.

Since Althusser both defended this theoretical realism
and supported the French Communits Party, some critics
say that his antihumanist account of Marx's development

defends communist dogma and oppression (See Aronowitz 180–81; Barrett 87–88; Fougeyrollas 20–22; Glucksman, "Marxism" 289; Jay 405, 411; and Marty 134–36). It is true that he remained a party member for his whole life, yet his account consistently opposes Stalinist and totalitarian views of communism. The reason is that in his account the scientific method presupposed by Marx's critique of Hegel divorces the object of experience from the object of knowledge. Scientific theory preserves the relative autonomy of its field and methods, while ideology imposes the traditional "dialectical unity" of principles ("theory") and practice or ideas and facts. Totalitarian theorists, who consider the dialectical unity of scientific truth and political practice a profoundly irrational and dogmatic "groupthink," argue that this unity enables a "disciplined party" to ensure the "revolutionary fulfillment" of its doctrines and the "violent" elimination of all dissent and resistance (see Brzezinski and Friedrich 87, and Krancberg 56). Althusser, by contrast, considers all versions of this unity a humanist myth. For this reason, Carl Freedman says, "no other theoretical approach could so stubbornly resist both official" Stalinism and its humanist "inversions" (Freedman 1990, 322).

Other critics rightly object that Althusser's account of Marx's development fails to identify the specific point at which Marx's new science breaks with Hegelian humanism and that the account betrays the rationalist's unduly optimistic belief that some preordained harmony brings nature and reason together (see Aronowitz 180–81; Glucksman, "Marxism" 289; and Smith, *Althusser* 97). Still other critics accept Althusser's rationalist account of science but fear that his account of ideological interpellation imposes a robotlike, "functionalist" conformity with established discourse (Montag, "Marxism" 72; Hirst, *Law*, 43–46). In an influential formulation, Paul Hirst says that the ideological apparatus can only reproduce the social relations of capitalist society if this apparatus ensures the unity of ruling class ideology. The unity of the ruling class, in turn, preserves the unity of its ideology and of the ideological apparatus. As a consequence, the ideological apparatus reduces intellectuals to structural supports of ruling-class ideology (*Law* 50–51).

An objection to this critique is that, following Gramsci, Althusser divides the power of the state from the state apparatus. State power is what a distinct class exercises, whereas state apparatuses, which include repressive structures (courts, legislatures, prisons, police, army) and ideological structures (political parties, schools, media, churches, families) are what intellectuals run. State power is a political matter bearing on who does or does not rule a country, while ideological state apparatuses are a structural matter reproducing social relations. Hirst admits that Althusser preserves the formal autonomy of the ideological state aparatus, but Hirst still argues that Althusser's persistent "economism" requires the ideological state apparatuses to function as agents ensuring ruling class unity (*Law* 43–44). This argument assumes that, as agents, the state apparatuses realize a unifying intention imposed by the ruling class. However, as I show in the next chapter, Althusser's account of the ideological apparatuses approximates Foucault's anti-intentionalist view, which maintains that the disciplinary technologies governing the body reproduce themselves or their institutions but do not enforce ruling-class ends and aims.

Moreover, in the later *Reading Capital*, where he distinguishes between philosophy and science, he goes on to repudiate the "foundational" rationalism of *For Marx*. Like Foucault, who rejects the humanist grounds of a discourse's truth, he says that he does not seek any such guarantees. He does not give up the idea that theory grasps reality, but he denies that theory reduces practice to a slavish instrument of an autonomous mind. He argues that theory follows its own practices, and practice presupposes its own theory.

To an extent, this criticism of foundational truths simply denies the dogmatic Stalinist belief that philosophical truth ensures political success. To a larger extent, this self-criticism suggests that epistemological norms do not enable philosophy to establish the scientific status of any or all theories. As Althusser says, Marx rejected "every philosophical ideology of the subject" because it "gave classical bourgeois philosophy the means of *guaranteeing* its ideas, practices, and goals" (Althusser, *Essays* 178). Stephen Resnick and Richard Wolff rightly suggest that this criticism of traditional epistemology parallels Richard Rorty's antifoundational account of them (Resnick and Wolff, *Knowledge* 17–19, 94–95). That is, Rorty rejects the traditional epistemological norms defended by classical philosophy and accepts the diverse discourses engaged in the philosophical "conversation"; Althusser too rejects science's unifying truth on transcendent grounds and acknowledges a discourse's diverse epistemologies. As Resnick and Wolff say, "[T]ruths, then, vary with the theories in and by which they are produced. There is no inter-theoretic standard of truth" ("Althusser's Liberation" 65).

Althusser claims, in addition, that in philosophical realms theory adopts partisan stances representing a subjective or "relativist" commitment to the class struggle. As he explains,

> [I]f the philosophy of philosophers is this perpetual war (to which Kant wanted to put an end by introducing the everlasting peace of his own philosophy), then no philosophy can exist within this theoretical relation of force except in so far as it marks itself off from its opponents and lays seige to that part of the positions which they have had to occupy in order to guarantee their power. (*Essays* 166)

Unlike Kant, who believed that reason overcomes the "antinomies" of the mind and imposes peace on warring philosophical schools, Althusser does not reduce philosophical schools to mere antinomies or demand that the schools accept a "rational" consensus opposing relativism or nominalism; rather, he maintains that,

> if philosophy is in the last instance class struggle at the level of theory, the politics which constitute philosophy bear on . . . a quite different question: *that of*

the ideological hegemony of the ruling class, whether
it is a question of organizing it, strengthening it,
defending it, or fighting against it. (*Essays* 167)

Balibar rightly says that Althusser's notion of class
struggle in theory does not preserve the realism of the early
theory, but the notion also does not justify liberal views or
express hostility to Marxism; rather, this notion opens the
"relativist" conventions of the social sciences or the humanities to political critique. Consider a difficult case: *The Postmodern Condition*, in which Jean-François Lyotard says that
the "grand narratives" in which God, the class struggle, or
social progress explain historical change can no longer justify the technocracy (60). Many scholars call this work anti-
thetical to Marxism because it considers modern discourses
relativist or incommensurable;[2] however, this work clearly
has post-Marxist import. In "La Place de l'alienation dans le
retournement Marxiste" ("The Place of Alienation in the
Marxist Transformation" ([1969]), an early essay that re-
sponds to the 1960s political upheavals, Lyotard grants Althusser's claim that the scientific theory discovered by Karl
Marx establishes its formal independence of its sociohistorical context. Lyotard also accepts Althusser's belief that the
scientific theory of Marx discovers, undermines, and opposes
Hegelian theory. Lyotard argues, however, that Marx rejects
Feuerbach's Hegelian negation or destruction of particular
spaces or realities because, close to the Frankfurt School, Lyotard considers alienated labor an oppositional force, rather
than a vestige of Hegelian humanism, as Althusser claimed.

In other words, Lyotard admits that the capitalist economy and its state bureacracy grant science the formal autonomy defended by Althusser; however, while Althusser
examines how the "ideological apparatus of the state" re-
produces itself, Lyotard argues that in Marx's account the
state and the economy work together to circulate and reproduce capital. He maintains that science does not resist ideology; science fosters and defends the reproduction of
capital and the exploitation of workers, teachers, and students. In the former USSR and in the Western world the

growth of economic exploitation and of the technocratic state bureaucracy has given the sciences, including Marxism, a conservative function: they justify the capitalist economic enterprises and the state bureaucracy and alienate both workers and students.

While Althusser considers alienation a vestige of Hegelian humanism, Lyotard emphasizes the traditional alienation of students and workers and opposes the capitalist and communist state bureaucracy and the Communist Party's dogmatic views and conservative functions. In *The Postmodern Condition* (1979), Lyotard still grants Althusser's belief that the various sciences establish and preserve their formal autonomy, but he goes on to reject Hegelian Marxism, which he now identifies with the technocracy. Construing this identification as a feature of a new or "postmodern" era, he argues that the technocracy faces a legitimation crisis: the "grand narratives" in which God, the class struggle, or social progress explain historical change can no longer justify the technocracy (60). In Wittgenstein's positivist or analytic terms, he says that the cognitive, prescriptive and evaluative "forms of life" or "language games" of the sciences expect their performance or competence, not the grand narratives, to legitimate them. In other words. Lyotard takes the specialized sciences or disciplines to provide their own legitimating "ideological" rationales because the traditional grand narratives can no longer justify them ("le <petit récit> reste la forme par excellence que prend l'invention imaginative, et tout d'abord dans la science" [98]). Althusser also says that, to establish formal autonomy, science denies that the grand teleological histories of the humanist tradition or the universal norms of human reason explain a science's importance or ground the specialized disciplines; however, Lyotard critiques the sciences on broad humanist grounds—formally incommensurate, the cognitive, prescriptive, and evaluative language games of the disciplines fail to comprehend such horrifying evils as the Holocaust; Althusser, who claims that the sciences face unending conflicts with their enabling ideologies, adopts the partisan stance that the disciplines' divisions represent class or political differences.

Althusserian Post-Marxism: From Étienne Balibar to Stephen Resnick and Richard Wolff

Balibar acknowledges this postmodern import of Althusser's later views but condemns their relativist or partisan character. He grants that Althusser faulted his initial science/ideology opposition and his foundational "theoreticism" and redefined philosophy as "class struggle in theory." In an ad hominem manner, Balibar argues, however, that, since Althusserian concepts such as "antihumanism" "or "reproduction" contain their oppositions within them, Althusser's self-criticism shows a suicidal, self-destructive drive, as his subsequent murder of his wife Hélène indicates (*Écrit* 68–73). For example, Balibar reduces Althusser's political dilemmas to a "schizophrenic situation, in which, although criticizing almost every aspect of . . . the [French] Communist organization and of . . . the bourgeois academic institution, he would consider it as an absolute necessity to remain a member of the organization and to work in the institution" ("Structural" 113). Balibar claims that, as a result, Althusser blurred his "decisive break with epistemological relativism" and reintroduced a "'class determination' of the 'lines of demarcation in theory.'"[3] In other words, to preserve the conceptual truth and scientific objectivity of the still "rational" Althusser, Balibar says that "genuine" Althusserian theory "takes its distance from any form of 'constructivism' or relativism, even in the sophisticated form given it by Foucault" (Balibar, "Object" 163; see also Nelson 166–67; Resch, *Althusser* 166; Smith, *Reading* 81–82 and 215; Sprinker, "Current Conjuncture" 829–31).

Resnick and Wolff, who, along with Anthony Callari, David Ruccio, and others, organized the Rethinking Marxism collective, also defend the conceptual truth of Marxism, but they maintain that, far from suicidal or schizophrenic, Althusser successfully critiques his earlier rationalist science and adopts a justified partisan stance, which establishes what they call the "Althusserian standpoint" and I term post-Marxist theory: "[I]t is possible and, from an Althusserian standpoint, necessary to interrogate every theory in terms of its social conditions and its social consequences.

Indeed, what a Marxian epistemology does is to erect those conditions and consequences as its criteria of the acceptability of all existing theories, i.e., its partisan attitude toward them"("Althusser's Liberation" 67). Although Resnick and Wolff grant that, as Balibar charges, Althusser's partisan account of philosophical schools or movements has the relativist import that also characterizes Foucault's histories or Lyotard's language games, Resnick and Wolff still argue that Althusserian theory goes beyond relativism: its "'relativist' commitment to the plurality of theories and their truths is merely the prelude for the specification of their partisan positions" (*Knowledge* 36).

Resnick and Wolff forcefully demonstrate, moreover, that Althusser's account of Marx's theories undermines traditional empiricist and rationalist epistemologies, especially their reductive insistence that the plain economic facts or the underlying historical realities ground legitimate theory (82–89). Plain fact or an absolute historical ground does not overcome the multiplicity or diversity of discourse because the conceptual processes of diverse discourses are influenced or "overdetermined" by social life's many facets. As a result, Althusser's account undermines not only empiricist and rationalist epistemologies but also all essentialist theories, including the traditional opposition between materialism and idealism as well as reductive notions of cause and effect or appearance and reality.

Resnick and Wolff grant that Althusser inconsistently preserved economic determinism in the famous "last instance"; they argue, however, that, since he considered the whole an overdetermined structure in which each part, event, or process influences every other, he effectively repudiated such economic and epistemological essentialism and initiated a post-Marxist or Marxian epistemology (*Knowledge* 93–95). They still claim, however, that Marxian theory "is motivated by, focused upon, and aims at an ever-deeper knowledge of" society's "economic aspects and, in particular, the class processes and their interrelationships" (*Knowledge* 96–97). Since, like Balibar, they redefine class processes in terms of the production and distribution of surplus value, not one's position in a social hierarchy, the overdetermined character of social processes allows them many subjects or "subsumed classes"; at the same time, this traditional focus on the economy denies that these processes have many subjects—economic, cultural, political, theological—and, as a result, a unified or central subject. Instead, they assimilate to class position the racial, sexual, or ethnic identities which other post-Marxists consider independent of class orientation. Class position admits questions of identity or issues of race and gender only insofar as different groups suffer different kinds of appropriation or exploitation (see *Class and its others*).

In addition, in *Class Theory and History*, Resnick and Wolff say that central to communism are class processes, which are a question of who produces and distributes surplus value, not who owns property or exercises power. They say that in a communist society, the producers of surplus value also distribute it; in a capitalist society, those who appropriate and distribute surplus value are different from those who produce it (14). As a result, a communist society can be based on private ownership of property, decentralized state powers, and competitive markets, just as a capitalist society can be run by the state and based on centralized state powers and a planned economy (51–79). Indeed, Resnick and Wolff argue that, despite some early, agricultural communism, the USSR developed state capitalism, not communism:

> The USSR . . . changed the form of the capitalist class organization from a private to a state capitalism. For example, in place of private boards of directors appropriating the surplus produced by industrial workers, the USSR substituted state officials as the appropriators. The mass of industrial workers . . . produced a surplus appropriated by others and distributed by the latter to still others. (xii)

Even though the USSR provided industrial and other workers the freedoms and benefits of a socialist society, these workers "produced a surplus appropriated" and distributed by others, so the USSR developed and maintained state capitalism.

While this account is sound, Resnick and Wolff conclude that, if the USSR had not ignored these class processes, it would not have suffered such disasters: "The costs of conceptual blindness toward the organization of surplus labor proved extremely heavy" (13). Doesn't this conclusion overstate the import of conceptual analysis? Would clarifying what communist class processes entailed for industry or the household have mitigated the "costs" of the Stalinist dictatorship, whose roots lie, as I indicated in the introduction, in the Russia's czarist bureaucracy, Lenin's elitist party, collectivization of agriculture, and so on?

Certainly Resnick and Wolff know very well that the Stalinist dictatorship had such different causes; still, what their emphasis on class processes suggests is that, even though they forcefully defend Althusser's critique of his earlier rationalism and his partisan account of philosophical movements, they preserve a rationalist style of conceptual elaboration. Like Descartes, who finds his key notions within himself, they reformulate Marxist theory as a matter of the "production, deployment, and organization of concepts" (*Knowledge* 2) and thereby preserve the rationalist opposition between philosophy and rhetoric, concepts and figural devices, truth and history.[4] While Resnick and Wolff grant that Althusser faults the theoreticism presupposed by the science/ideology distinction, they reduce the distinction to mere pejorative labeling (*Knowledge* 94) and ignore the historical evolution whereby distinct discourses develop a science or a formal method from their equally distinct ideological contexts.

As I will argue in the next chapter, Althusser's account of a science's or discourse's evolution parallels that of Foucault, who rejects the distinction of science/ideology but traces the historical evolution of particular discourses in great detail. Moreover, post-Marxist theorists such as Laclau and Mouffe and Judith Butler move beyond not only rationalism and empiricism but also the Platonic opposition of concepts and rhetoric. In sum, while Althusser's defense of a scientific Marxism effectively undermines the Hegelian and/or totalitarian import of traditional Marxism and produces a partisan critique of philosophy's schools or movements, he too did not pursue such rhetorical analyses not only because he preserved the traditional notion of economic determination in the last instance but also because he shared the traditional contempt of academia. In the autobiography he admits that he considered his life as a teacher and a scholar nothing more than "endless artifice and deceit . . . totally inauthentic" (277; see also Rancière, "La Scène" 65). He even imagined that, since his wife fervently believed in him, his murdering her would show the world his true inauthenticity; as he says, "The best way of proving you do not exist is to destroy yourself by destroying the person who loves you and above all believes in your *existence*" (283; see also 276).

_____

Chapter 2

From Archaeology
to Genealogy

Michel Foucault and
Post-Marxist Histories

Foucault examines the breakdown of phenomenology, not Marxism, whose limits, he says, the study of the Gulag exposes (Foucault, *Power/Knowledge* 134–37); nonetheless, like Althusser, he suggests that, contrary to foundational, humanist ideals, the discourses of the disciplines or power/knowledge impose ideals of normality and thereby reproduce themselves and/or the subject. Althusser too claims that, constituting or interprellating the subject, ideology is rooted in institutional rituals that reproduce it ("Ideology" 166), but he argues that, opposed to ideology, science independently develops its concepts and does not conform with practice, fact, or truth (*For Marx* 182–93). Foucault, who considers science "one practice among many," repudiates this opposition and explains discourses' positive, factual history, including their gaps and ruptures. As a consequence, while Althusser preserves traditional notions of economic determination and working-class or communist party politics, Foucault's genealogies of punishment or sexuality implicitly foster the politics of marginal groups, what feminists and post-Marxists term a radical coalition of women's, black, and other "new social movements" (see Lois McNay 111 and Janet Sawicki, *Disciplining* 8–10).

Some critics esteem the subjective, local character of Foucault's histories but fault his notion that the discourses of power/knowledge constitute a normal subject because they fear that in a functionalist manner this view, like Althusser's account of ideological interpellation, leaves too little room for resistance.[1] The exception is Foucault's last works, which maintain that the strategies and tactics whereby males regulated their bodies and thereby assured the health of their souls differed markedly in the classical Greek and in the Christian eras (see Ingram 237 and McNay 3, 87); however, I won't say much about these works, which do not show much Althusserian influence. They discuss the constitution of the self, not the strategies or tactics of modern discursive technologies nor the social or institutional changes that explain their evolution.

Other critics grant that Foucauldian accounts of a discourse's history and normative import subvert ruling-class ends and aims but deny that Marxism has very much to do with these accounts.[2] It is true that in the relatively early *Madness and Civilization* Foucault emphasizes the Nietzschean notion that discourse does not uncover a preexistent object; discourse constitutes the objects, including the human "object," which it purports to uncover. In the early, Nietzschean mode, he parodies the pretentious objectivity of positivist medical or psychological disciplines and esteems the power of madness, the disciplines' silent and repressed other, to transgress their ethical and social norms.[3] In this early and in later work, Foucault also argues, however, that, like the medical historians who discover in ancient treatises examples of modern pathologies or neuroses, scientists treat the forms of madness as eternal and unchanging, but actually the changed, institutional arrangements of the eighteenth and the nineteenth centuries explain the changing forms that madness takes. Pierre Macherey, Tony Bennett, and Toby Miller rightly suggest that this claim is Althusserian (see chapters 5 and 6). That is, even though Althusser speaks of ideology and not of particular discourses, he too claims that, constituting or interprellating the subject, ideology is rooted in institutional rituals that reproduce it.

In later works, Foucault examines not only these "archaeological" forms but also the "genealogical" import of a discourse, whose power to constitute a subject extends to the individual as well as the "social" subject. He still shows, however, that, organizing and reorganizing social life, the established discourses of "power/knowledge" constitute the "normal" subject" but preserve their autonomy and ubiquity, instead of serving the ends and aims of the ruling class.[4] Although this genealogical view repudiates the theoretical critique defended by Laclau and Mouffe and Butler, the view implicitly fosters what they consider the radically democratic politics of oppositional women's, black, or ethnic movements.

In the early *Madness and Civilization*, Foucault claims that discourse about madness imposes and violates middle-class norms, rather than constituting a subject or organizing society. Like Nietsche, who preserves the ancient view that that Dionysiac madness is a tragic experience, Foucault shows that madness readily transgresses the ethical precepts of "bourgeois" morality, but, to oppose the Kantian notion that the human subject imposes transcendental forms of understanding (see Béatrice Han 64–65), he maintains the changing historical contexts of madness explain this transgression (*histoire de la folie* 85). For example, he says that in the fifteenth and the sixteenth centuries madness replaces leprosy as a spiritual condition revealing signs of God's wisdom. Like the lepers, the mad, who are on a voyage, a quest, or a journey, remain within the community, where madness shows the tragic abyss of life, its existential emptiness; however, in the seventeenth and eighteenth century the rationalists condemn madness as error and exclude it from social life. "Reason" excludes madness from itself and from society because the mad can always overcome their insanity and think rationally. The many hospitals and workhouses built by the seventeenth century grouped together sexual libertines, debauchers, alchemists, victims of venereal disease, impious disbelievers, homosexuals, and the mad on the grounds that all such abnormal activities simply violated ethical and theological norms.

Foucault suggests that it was not scientific critique or outraged humanity but institutional changes that ended the practice of interning the mad with the criminals, vagabonds, and profligates. For example, in the late eighteenth and early nineteenth century, psychopathology returned the mad to human realms, but only because in this era the mad acquire human rights. Moreover, once economics becomes a distinct discipline, poverty loses its status as a moral fault. Since economics shows that the poor work to make the rich rich, society admits that it is obligated to help the laboring poor, and the poor and the mad are separated. Liberated from internment, the mad become free to enter asylums, where psychoanalysis, which becomes an absolute wisdom, gives it the power to speak, to end its silence, and to recognize itself.

Historians have objected that this account of madness misconstrues the extent, duration, and importance of these treatments;[5] such objections ignore or dismiss the account's philosophical import: to show that the historical context of institutions and beliefs explains the changing forms of treatment or medical discourse, not, as Kant claimed, the transcendental conditions of human understanding. In *The Order of Things,* Foucault also shows that changing historical conditions, not transcendental forms, explain the changing forms of discourse, but he does not elaborate the Nietzschean view that madness itself undermines the ethical norms of the rationality excluding it; rather, he adopts Gaston Bachelard's and Georges Canguilhem's belief that evolving paradigms explain the historical development of a science. Foucault assumes that such a paradigm or episteme underlies an era's disciplines or expert knowledges and explains their cognitive force. These epistemes are not worldviews realizing the predetermined telos of the world spirit, as Hegel would say, nor are they ideologies constituted and transformed by changing relations of production, as Marx would argue; rather, modes of positive knowledge, they rupture and break with each other. In positive histories, Foucault shows, moreover, that the Renaissance, the classical era, and the modern era constitute sets of assumptions or "epistemès" establishing the disciplines that subsequently undermine them.

For example, Foucault says that the knowledge and techniques of the Renaissance's episteme serve to interpret the resemblances suggested by linguistic signs. This interpretation guarantees that hermeneutics, which claims that the microcosm of linguistic signs mirrors the macrocosm of the world, provides knowledge of the world: as Foucault says, "The world is covered with signs which one must decipher, and these signs, which reveal resemblances and affinities, are themselves only forms of similitude. To know is then to interpret" (*Les mots et les choses* 47). He goes on to suggest that the classical episteme of the seventeenth and eighteenth century does not construe knowledge as the hermeneutic interpretation of signs uniting microcosm and macrocosm. Rather, this episteme establishes a relation between knowledge and "mathesis," a universal science of measure and order, not between words and the world. This relationship establishes, in turn, a number of empirical domains, including general grammar, natural history, and analysis of riches. As Foucault says, these new empirical disciplines "could not be constituted without the relationship which the whole episteme of western culture maintains with the universal science of order" ("Toutes ces empiricités . . . n'ont pu se constituer sans le rapport que toute l'*épistémé* de la culture occidentale a entretenu alors avec une science universel de l'ordre") (71).

Foucault says that the nineteenth century ruptures with this eighteenth-century pursuit of order. In place of an order that explains identities and differences, the nineteenth century substitutes a notion of history in which analogy explains the succession and arrangement of distinct organizations. The nineteenth century also substitutes the study of the familiar philology, biology, and political economy for the eighteenth century's strange study of language, riches, and history. In this way too, knowledge, which acquires new figures (production, life, language), has changed.

This archaeology of the modern disciplines does not examine their institutional changes, but it does show that the seventeenth, eighteenth, and nineteenth century epistemes influenced their development. Similarly, when Althusser rejects the broad distinction between theory and ideology, he argues that economics, history, philosophy, mathematics, science, and other disciplines and practices establish their own "inward" criteria of validity and produce their own legitimate objects and discourses. As a result, the disciplines create what Althusser calls a "knowledge effect," not cognitive truths nor autonomous facts (*Reading* 60–63). He means that the experts of a discipline consider a particular theory legitimate knowledge because the theory conforms with the discipline's "problematic," which is the conventions and discourses explaining why experts accept certain theories at one time and other theories at another time.

Moreover, just as Althusser critiques Hegelian or Marxist humanism, so Foucault claims that in the twentieth century the modern disciplines fracture the unified figure of human being in terms of which in the nineteenth century phenomenology grounds them. The modern episteme divides into the mathematical sciences, the social sciences, and philosophical disciplines and thereby undermines the phenomenological project—to establish the human foundation of the sciences. Phenomenology, which summarizes the nineteenth-century rupture with eighteenth-century discourse, describes lived experience as the "impensé" or non-thought; however, just as Nietzsche's proclaiming the death of God and the advent of the Superman means that man dies as well, so too does this non-thought mean the end of phenomenology's human-centered anthropology. Eric Marty rightly complains that Foucault inconsistently condemns the other or non-thought of humanist phenomenology but esteems the other (the Superman) of Nietzschean antihumanism (116–18); however, Marty, who considers the antihumanism of Althusser and Foucault an ahistorical, structuralist critique at best and at worst a neurotic rage against Sartre (110), argues that, highly original, phenomenology's vision of subjective life exceeds humanism and undermines all "objectivist rationality" (128). Foucault's point is, however, that, while formal versions of phenomenology may rigorously exclude historicism and psychologism, they cannot make the human sciences fit the divisions of the modern disciplines, which radically destablize them. Like Althusser, Foucault takes the modern disciplines to subvert traditional humanism but claims that, invented in the nineteenth century, humanity remains an effect of language, not, as phenomenology claims, a genuine foundation.

In *The Archaeology of Knowledge* (1969) he goes on to repudiate Hegelian humanism. He argues that contradiction has many levels and functions within and between discursive formations and does not represent a difference to be resolved or a fundamental principle of explanation (149–56). In *Reading Capital* (1968), Althusser also objects that Hegel's idealist dialectic imposes a self-identical telos preserving historical continuities and repressing historical ruptures. As Toby Miller says, Althusser examines the broad, social force of an ideological apparatus, while Foucault describes the disciplinary effects of diverse micropowers, but both of them speak of a "cite" or "social surface," rather than a totality (*Self* 33–35).

Moreover, Foucault complains that the Hegelian pursuit of a transcendental reality whose underlying or immanent opposition can mediate among different discourses defends "the sovereignty of the subject" against the "decentering operated by Marx—by the historical analysis of the relations of production, economic determinations, and the class struggle. . . . One is led . . . to anthropologize Marx, to make of him an historian of totalities, and to rediscover in him the message of humanism" (*Knowledge* 12–13). As I have noted in chapter 1, Althusser also opposes Marxist humanism, but Althusser claims that Marx rejects the humanist belief that "the real is the discourse of a voice," "the written" is "the transparency of the true," the sight reveals the unmediated truth of the world, and at history's end a flesh and blood person—"*this* bread, *this* body, *this* face and *this* man"—manifests the concept or spirit (*Reading* 16).

Fredric Jameson accepts these parallels of Foucault and "the Althusserians" but considers them dialectical despite their critiques of Hegelian humanism. That is, they both describe the evolution of incommensurable epistemes or combinations, and they both emphasize the gaps or ruptures whereby one displaces the other, rather than the continuities tying the new to the old (*Modernity* 78–79). As a result, they both show, Jameson says, the same weakness: in the Althusserian account, "the emergence of the new system remains as mythic and unaccountable, as uncaused and unprecedented, as in the case of Foucault's epistemes" (*Modernity* 80). Since Hegelian/Marxist humanism explains such change, this criticism implicitly assimilates their views to this humanism despite the many difficulties which, as I explained in the introduction, it faces.

Andrew Parker grants, by contrast, that they forcefully deconstruct Hegelian humanism, but Parker objects that, preserving scientific truth, Althusser does not accept the indeterminacy, free play, and difference of Derridean theory (59–60). Parker is right but not because of Althusser's scientific rationalism; rather, Althusser shares Foucault's notion of a discourse's authority or power. As Toby Miller says, they both consider the constitutive import of established discourses, ideologies, or "power/ knowledge" more important than figural import revealed by theoretical critique (*Self* 33–40).

In *Discipline and Punish,* Foucault goes on to argue, for example, that, as a strategy with dispositions and techniques, discourse forms a complex of power/knowledge organizing diverse institutions including the family. He still assumes that such complexes establish the domination but do not serve the interests of a dominant class, but, since he repudiates the Hegelian episteme underlying and unifying diverse discourses, he produces what he termed a genealogy of a discourse's divisions and influence, rather than an archaeology explaining an era's discourses about criminals, the insane, or knowledge. As Han points out, a geneology denies the relative autonomy of a discourse or discipline and examines instead its internal conflicts and external authority or social influence as well as the nexus or mutual elaboration of power and knowledge (123–27, 196–98; see also Poster *Foucault, Marxism, and History* 39). While

Althusser also repudiates Hegelian theory and examines a discipline's or science's history, especially its conflicts of ideology and theory, Althusser inconsistently retains the economy as an absent cause unifying disciplines and institutions. Because a genealogy of a discourse's conflicts, divisions, or ruptures more radically critiques the autonomy of discourse and denies its present configuration is inevitable or unalterable, the local geneologies may implicitly support prisoner or gay rights groups or what feminists and post-Marxists term "new social movements."

For instance, he points out that, to determine the culpability of the accused, judges require the expertise of psychiatrists, anthropologists, and criminologists, all of whom enable the judge to determine what the criminal can be, not just what he did. Exercised not only on the accused or the guilty but also on the insane, children, students, prisoners, workers, and ex-convicts, this scientific-juridical complex engages in political tactics and strategies producing what Foucault terms a technology of the body. Foucault still situates this genealogy in distinct historical periods whose sociohistorical changes explain its evolution, but the genealogy examines the emergence and extension of the technology, not the episteme underlying various discourses.

For example, the genealogy begins in the fifteenth and the sixteenth centuries, when legal punishment tortured the body, tracing on it the signs of power. Judges, who embodied the right of the sovereign to establish guilt or innocence, used torture to make people confess. Since any one accused of a crime was guilty to an extent, torture was considered both punishment and truth-producing. The justices could require the criminal to authenticate the torture by confessing and repenting his crimes because the pain of punishment affirmed the sovereign's power and superiority.

Foucault shows that, by contrast, the new penal system of the eighteenth century eliminates torture because torture, which required the presence of the people, becomes a sign of tyranny. Moreover, class differences in punishment provoke rebellion, and the people avenge themselves in blood. Instead of torture, the new penal system makes the person discovered in the criminal the object of reform, which adjusts punishment to individual characters. What Foucault calls this new "ideological power" involves a political anatomy in which the body is the principal actor. Punishment no longer avenges the outraged sovereign; punishment, which becomes public and certain, seeks to prevent the repetition of the crime. Natural, logical, punishment shows the immediacy of the laws, not the presence of the sovereign.

Foucault says, moreover, that in the nineteenth century the prison takes all aspects of the individual in charge. The reformatory prescribes a recoding of existence much different from the pure privation of liberty. Isolation assures remorse and total subjugation. The prisons teach the value of work and of property. The inmate becomes an object of knowledge, a delinquent whose biography shows his slow formation. The prison is the place in which the power to punish organizes a "field of objectivity" in which punishment can function as therapeutic. In Bentham's panopticon, a famous example, the prisoner is seen but does not see; the central tower sees but the guard in it is not seen. Power becomes automatic, a matter of observation. Moreover, a panopticon allows an observer to classify prisoners and to conduct tests on them. The maximum intensity of the panopticon's power is not in the ruler's body but in the individualized body produced by this observation and testing.

Like Foucault's earlier critiques of theory, these contrasts between punishment as the sovereign's revenge and punishment as observation and control also show that institutional changes, not scientific enlightenment or humanity, change the old, despotic system; however, these contrasts show that the disciplines of power and knowledge both objectify and dominate their subjects and thereby elaborate each other. Moreover, this genealogy of knowledge and power restates and revises Althusser's Gramscian distinction between the ideological apparatus of the state, which persuades individuals to accept ruling-class hegemony, and state power, which coerces them into accepting that hegemony.[6] Foucault argues that, impersonal and autonomous, a discipline is not a form of ideological hegemony but an "anatomy of power" used by different institutions including the family to impose conceptions of normality ensuring ruling-class domination; nonetheless, he points out that, while eighteenth-century philosophers and jurists seek in the legal pact the model on which to construct social life, the technicians of discipline elaborate techniques of individual and collective coercion of bodies. The eighteenth-century bourgeoisie, which becomes the dominant class, imposes a juridical code of formal equality and a parliamentary form of regime. Disciplines are the other side of these processes. Essentially inegalitarian and hierarchic, disciplinary systems of micropower underpin the general juridical form which guarantees an egalitarian system of rights.

Hierarchic surveillance, continual registration, perpetual judgment and classification—these are discipline's anonymous instruments. Foucault's most interesting example is the exam, which he considers a technique of continual surveillance invented by the eighteenth century. In the school or the hospital, the exam shows the subjugation of those perceived as objects and the objectification of those who are subjugated. Since exams require documents, records, and registers, they give rise to sciences that subjugate the people that they individualize. The rewards and the penalties of this disciplinary surveillance impose standards of normality on docile bodies. Disciplines adjust a "multiplicity" of people to the multiplying apparatuses of production, including the production of knowledge and of aptitudes at school, of health in hospitals, and of destructive force in the army. One cannot, Foucault argues, separate the accumulation of capital from the accumulation of people—the techniques that make the "cumulative multiplicity" of people useful accelerate the accumulation of capital.[7]

In other words, he suggests that, while the bourgeoisie imposes formal or legal equality, this "microphysics" of power, coercive, not persuasive, underpins eighteenth-century social life. Schools, hospitals, prisons, armies, and factories employ these technologies, which organize spaces, time, and bodies. As in the earlier works, Foucault claims here too that in the eighteenth-century hospital, school, factory, and prison, where the technologies ensure objectivation and subjugation, disciplinary procedures or mechanisms enable knowledge and power to reinforce each other. In other words, repudiating theoretical critique, he shows that, while the disciplines making up the human sciences seem to oppose and to change schools or factories, the disciplines actually make the technology more effective. Indeed, in the nineteenth and twentieth centuries, these technologies spread to so many different institutions that Foucault speaks of a whole carceral society, not just prisons. Moreover, he points out that, even though the prison fails to reform criminals, the prison remains the central form of punishment. The carceral society perpetuates the delinquency the prisons means to reduce because this society uses delinquency to survey the population and to direct and exploit tolerated illegalities. Taking even the least infraction to mean delinquency, this society effectively constructs a normal subject supporting ruling-class domination but not ruling-class ends.

In *The History of Sexuality* (vol.1), Foucault also shows that, as strategies of power, disciplinary knowledge has a constitutive or "subjectivizing" force whereby it enables or "interpellates" the subject, including its unconscious. In this case, he claims, however, that sexual desire is not repressed or subversive, as Freudians and Marxists say; it is a normal construct of modern discourses, which incessantly promote talk about sex: as he says,

> From the singular imperialism that compels everyone to transform their sexuality into a perpetual discourse, to the manifold mechanisms which, in the areas of economy, pedagogy, medicine, and justice, incite, extract, distribute, and institutionalize the sexual discourse, an immense verbosity is what our civilization has acquired and organized. Surely no other type of society has ever accumulated . . . a similar quantity of discourses concerned with sex (33).

Modern society talks so obsessively about sex not because sexuality has been repressed but because society evolves a will-to-knowledge about sexual matters. As I show in the next two chapters, Laclau and Mouffe and Butler say that, while the rituals and practices of an established ideology construct or "interpellate" the subject but repress his or her subversive desires, critical theory resists this repression and liberates the subject,[8] whereas, because of this "immense verbosity," Foucault rejects what he calls the "juridico-discursive" view shared by the Marxist account of ideology and the Freudian account of parental law and childhood's instincts. Those accounts accept the conventional theory that the Victorian era repressed sexual activity on moral or theological grounds, while modern society is open, liberated, or free because it allows pornography, birth control, abortion, frank sexual talk, unmarried couples, homosexual relationships, strip joints, etc.; actually, since the medieval era, society has revealed a Nietzschean will-to-knowledge about sex. Scholars consider Foucault anti-Marxist; nonetheless, in *The History of Madness*, the Nietzschean will to power transgressed bourgeois morality, while, in the *History of Sexuality*, the will-to-knowledge is embedded in institutional practices, especially the confession.

Foucault points out, for example, that in the medieval era, the church demanded very detailed confessions of sexual acts, whereas in the seventeenth century confession shifts from such explicit acts to more private thoughts and intentions. He says that the eighteenth and nineteenth centuries make the confession a principal form of truth and the basis of a science of sex which requires the confession of sexual activity, desires, thoughts, etc. The listener is an authority as well as an interpreter. Sex is not condemned but urged to speak and to be interpreted.

More importantly, he shows that in the eighteenth and nineteenth centuries governmental policies, which regulate population, birth control, and sexual hygiene and education, explain sexual activities and thereby produce discussions of sex at the same time that they police the activities of the population. For instance, the science of eugenics meant the sterilization of "undesireables" (perverts, etc.), so that they could not perpetuate their faults. Medical discourse also makes homosexuality a perversion. More than a couple, the conjugal family has scientific technicians prescribing proper sexual conduct and networks of servants and children regulating it. In the nineteenth century, for example, parents regulated a child's masturbation, as psychologists urged them to.

In this way Foucault once again critiques theoretical ideals, for it is the normalizing practices established in the family or other institutions, not in the law nor in scientific or humanist theory, that explain the changes in social life; this time, however, he claims that power both proliferates pleasure and multiplies perversions or misconducts. He shows, for instance, that power produces the figures of the hysterical woman, the masturbating child, the Malthusian couple, and the perverse adult. Similarly, psychology, medicine, etc. give the middle class its own body, while welfare, birth control, poverty, etc. give the working class a different body. Hence, Foucault claims that sexuality is not the means whereby the bourgeoisie co-opts the working class, as the Frankfurt School says; on the contrary, the working class develops its own sexuality because it finds bourgeois sexuality oppressive. Lastly, medical discourse claimed that pure blood ties excluded mixed marriages—no miscegenation—while perversion resulted from degenerate family lines—an insane parent, etc. Since racism stems from this nineteenth-century union of pure blood and bourgeois sexuality, Foucault's account of sexuality ultimately explains the Holocaust.

Unlike the archaeological accounts of madness and knowledge, the genealogical studies of punishment and sexuality examine the nexus of power/knowledge and radically critique the normative import of theoretical ideals; still, both the archaeological and the genealogical studies indicate that, rooted in institutional practices, discourse undermines the humanist's ideals of rational norms and universal truth and evolves distinct historical configurations that oppose ruling-class aims but still regulate the body, institutions, and even society. While these positive, factual studies do not explicitly promote a radical, democratic politics, the conflicts and divisions that the genealogical histories of punishment and sexuality reveal suggest that the present configurations of power/knowledge are not necessary and inevitable and thereby justify local, political coalitions subverting patriarchal norms of gendered identity, as feminists have shown.[9]

Gayatri Spivak argues, by contrast, that Foucault's notion of power cannot be understood in terms of this "radical democracy," which she identifies with liberal humanism. She claims that, far from critiquing the norms of theory, the genealogical studies continue the archaeological pursuit of what she terms "ontic-ontotheological" grounds: "For both Foucault and Derrida, in different ways, the ontico-ontological difference is a thinking through of the uses and the limits of a critical philosophy" (147). She denies that genealogical study has positive, political import because it must "think through . . . the uses and limits of a critical philosophy." By contrast, as I indicate in chapter 4, Judith Butler develops the Foucauldian notion that the norms of gender impose a performance constituting one's gender but argues that, since marginal groups interpellate these norms, this notion promotes the democratic politics of marginal groups. To clarify what such a politics actually entails, I turn in the next chapter to Laclau and Mouffe's original account.

Chapter 3

Post-Marxism and Democracy

The Political Theory of Ernesto Laclau and Chantal Mouffe

Foucault's archaeological and genealogical studies both indicate that, rooted in institutional practices, discourse evolves distinct configurations which oppose ruling class aims but still regulate the body, institutions, and even society. This contingent, historical view of discourse repudiates the Althusserian opposition of science and ideology and fosters, at least implicitly, a democratic coalition of women's, African American, postcolonial, gay, working-class, and other "new social movements." Well known as proponents of such a democratic coalition, Laclau and Mouffe also repudiate the Althusserian opposition. They too maintain that the discursive conflicts by which contending political parties seek to impose their hegemony explain values and identities more fully than ruling-class interests or social structures do; however, Laclau and Mouffe explain the "hegemonic" ideological practices constructing modern political identities, not the technologies regulating the body or society. Étienne Balibar, Alain Badiou, and other antihumanists repudiate such "identity politics" and defend the scientific rationalism of the early Althusser. By contrast, Laclau and Mouffe dismiss both the conceptual truth and scientific neutrality defended by rationalist philosophy and the discourses of power/knowledge disciplining the subject and in a Derridean fashion emphasize the subversive potential of theoretical critique. Unlike Judith Butler, who, as I indicate in the next chapter, accepts both the Derridean critique and the Foucauldian disciplinary technology, Laclau and Mouffe reduce the normalizing configurations of knowledge and power to "functional requirements" of the Althusserian "logic of reproduction" and ignore or deny the institutional determination of discourse. As a result, the post-Marxism of Laclau and Mouffe forcefully undermines the hegemonic ideologies whereby ruling blocs depict their values and interests as natural or universal and justifies excluded but not established women's, African American, gay, or working-class groups, political parties, organizations, or movements.

Like Althusser, Laclau and Mouffe critique the Hegelian belief that predetermined historical stages or economic contexts explain social development; however, while Althusser remained committed to the working class and its parties, Laclau complains that traditional Marxism treats the working class as a privileged agent achieving "full presence" in a "transparent" communist society. Althusser faults the foundational rationalism of Hegelian Marxism but preserves economic determination in the last instance, whereas Laclau claims that Marxist "rationalist naturalism" preserves the apocalyptic ideals of the Christian theology that Marxism opposes. That is, Christian theology maintains that the sacrifice of God overcomes evil and redeems humanity but situates the historical process of salvation beyond human understanding. Traditional Marxism considers the working class the agent of human salvation and the historical process a secular, scientific matter, but in a theological manner Marxism also expects the working class to overcome class conflict and establish a classless society (see *New Reflections* 76–78 and *Emancipation(s)* 9–15).

This critique of Hegelian Marxism effectively extends Althusser's critique of Hegelian Marxism's theological character. So does Laclau and Mouffe's version of Althusser's belief that the ideological apparatuses of the state interpellate or construct a subject and, thereby, reproduce themselves. Their version elaborates Antonio Gramsci's claim that the ideological hegemony of ruling elites explains a society's political formations. As Laclau points out, this view of hegemony is implicit in Marx's work, which says that the ruling class justifies its rule by construing its particular interests as universal; however, while Marx expected the growing simplification of history to reveal the working class' unmediated universality, Gramsci recognized the illusion of such unmediated universality and defended the contingent hegemonic universality of particular interests and local representations (Butler et al. 45–51). Lastly, Laclau and Mouffe's version of ideological interpellation adopts the poststructuralist belief that, since objects do not simply or literally mirror their sociohistorical contexts, the distinction between object and context, discursive and nondiscursive practices, or "thought and reality" breaks down; in Laclau and Mouffe's terms, "[s]ynonomy, metonomy, metaphor . . . are part of the primary terrain itself in which the social is constituted" (*Hegemony* 110).

On these poststructuralist grounds, Laclau and Mouffe make their central claim: that the discursive conflicts by which contending political parties seek to impose their hegemony explain values and identities more fully than ruling-class interests or social structures do.[1] As the modern assimilation of the working class implies, contradictions between classes can be harmonious, not violently emotional or oppositional. What exposes the fissures within hegemonic ideological practices is not, then, the conflict of classes but the antagonisms of women, minorities, gays, and others. The conflicts and struggles of these social movements undermine hegemonic literal meanings and conservative identities and justify those movements' assertion of democratic ideals. In Laclau's poststructuralist terms, hegemonic ideological discourses construct stable but partial or dislocated subjects whose antagonisms or dislocations ensure that they fail to achieve the "full presence" or closure sought by both Marxism and Christianity. As negativity, antagonism or dislocation does not imply a positive new context or "aufhebung," as the traditional Hegelian notion of negativity does; rather, antagonisms keep hegemonic ideological practices or social relations from constructing the literal import, full identity, and contradictory forces reflecting history's predetermined stages.

In later work, Laclau argues that the Lacanian notion of the unsymbolizable real explains the limits of identity formation. As a formal bar or limit, the Lacanian real ensures that no hegemonic block fully realizes the identities that its imposes. Since the subject remains fissured in either case, the antagonism of diverse social groups or the dislocation of social structures matters more than the systematic contradictions and predetermined structures of the traditional view (*Hegemony* 122–34).

The conservative John Ellis objects that the Soviet tragedy discredits "race-gender-class critics" because they critique the establishment in Rousseau's fashion but ignore the critique's historical consequences: totalitarian communism (12–32). Laclau and Mouffe do critique the establishment in this fashion but, unlike other Marxists, do not ignore the import of the Soviet experience.[2] On the contrary, they maintain that the tragic Soviet experience illustrates and justifies their claim that hegemonic discourse, rather than socioeconomic contexts, constructs the identity of the subject.

Laclau and Mouffe accept, in particular, the totalitarian theorist's belief that Marx's scientific view of history explains the Stalinist character of Soviet communism as well as the liberal historians' claim that, more than Marxist theory, Russian socioeconomic conditions explain Soviet Stalinism. On the one hand, Laclau and Mouffe say that the Soviet Party grew more and more dictatorial because Leninist theory gave the party the exclusive possession of the scientific truth and the exclusive right to define and to represent the working class and its interests (*Hegemony* 56–57); similarly, in the very influential *Totalitarian Dictatorship and Autocracy* (1956), Zbiginew Brzezinski and Carl J. Friedrich say that the rational ideals that Marx acquired from the French Enlightenment provided communism's key ideas, such as "total democracy," "rationalistic" revolution, and absolute political unanimity (82–83). Brzezinski and Friedrich show that Marx's ideas explain communism's totalitarian characteristics—a dogmatic ideology sanctioned by the state, a monolithic party ruled by a dictator, a terroristic system of police control, and a monopoly of communications, arms and weapons, and economic production (56).

Unlike Laclau and Mouffe, the totalitarian theorists go on, however, to reduce communism to an irrational other whose violations of democracy, science, and reason discredit not only Marxist theorists but also liberal, radical, or oppositional intellectuals.[3] Brzezinski and Friedrich emphasize, for example, the fanatic irrationality of the former Soviet state; in their terms, it substitutes "faith for reason, magic exhortation for scientific knowledge" (13).[4]

On empirical or "operational" grounds, Brzezinski and Friedrich assume, on the one hand, that communist violence, propaganda, and dictatorship show what Marxist theories of class struggle, ideological beliefs, and one-party rule really imply. Brzezinski and Friedrich claim, on the other, that blind, mystical faith in Marxist ideology explains Soviet terror and oppression. Since the operational rule whereby the Soviet practice of terror and oppression tells us the practical import of Marxist theory does not logically square with the cynical insistence that blind faith in Marxist ideology explains Soviet terror and oppression, these theorists face a blatant contradiction. To resolve it, they reject Marxism's claim that it provides both a scientific explanation of society and a practical guide to action. More precisely, they construe the dialectical unity of scientific truth and political practice as a profoundly irrational practice. As I indicated, Althusser treats this unity as a humanist myth, but they argue that, as the central dogma of nineteenth- and twentieth-century Marxism, this "groupthink" enables a "disciplined party" to ensure the "revolutionary fulfillment" of its doctrines and the "violent" elimination of all dissent and resistance (87; see also Krancberg 56).

Laclau and Mouffe reject this depiction of communism as an irrational other but grant that Marxist theory explains the dictatorial character of the Soviet Communist Party. On the other hand, Laclau and Mouffe accept the liberal historians' claim that, more than Marxist theory, Russian socioeconomic conditions explain the Stalinist system. More precisely, Laclau and Mouffe say that Stalinism brought together a feudal peasantry, an industrial working class, Czarist bureaucrats, and various other groups belonging to very different historical stages but deny that the continuity with the czar's feudal system explains the growth of Stalinism.

Liberal Russian historians such as Robert Tucker, Robert Daniels, and others say that, more than Marxist theory or Enlightenment reason, Russian conditions, including the authoritarian character of the peasantry and the socioeconomic difficulties of the late nineteenth century, explain the growth of the Stalinist system. For example, in *The Making of the Soviet System* Moshe Lewin points out that at that time the rural nexus of noble lords and religious peasants prevented the capitalist market from industrializing society. In 1917, when Lenin and the Bolsheviks came to power, Russia was predominantly rural, but the Bolsheviks, mainly professional revolutionaries, were supported largely by a precarious alliance of the small working class and the rural peasantry. By the middle 1920s, the civil war decimated the working class, the middle-class professionals, and the industrial plants and markets; growing increasingly hostile, the peasantry retreated into primitive, semiautonomous communes; and the Bolshevik party and Russian society grew more distant. To overcome this terrible isolation, the party recruited the czar's former bureaucrats as well as the uneducated, religious peasants. Lewin, Robert Tucker, and others claim that, as a consequence of this new membership and the fearful socioeconomic difficulties, the party grew much more intolerant and autocratic. Thus, to industrialize quickly, the Stalinists imposed collective farming on a hostile peasantry, liquidated the kulaks (rich peasants), and purged agricultural and industrial specialists. With the secret police built up to control an uncooperative peasantry, the Stalinists killed off the Bolsheviks and gradually adopted Imperial Russia's medieval practices, including the Czar's belief in "revolution from above"(Lewin, *The Making* 12–45, and *Gorbachev* 13–82; see also Tucker 61–71, 94–104; and Cohen 38–70). The Stalinists did some good: they changed the backward, agricultural USSR to a progressive, urban society, with many large cities, an educated population, and a public culture (Lewin 1988, 30–82; see also Daniels 67–69); nonetheless, Stalin's tyrannical regime came to approximate the equally tyrannical regimes of the eighteenth- and nineteenth-century czars, who also built huge projects, forced the peasants into slave labor camps, censored the work of artists and intellectuals, established a strong, modernizing central government, and organized an extensive secret police and a highly ritualized bureaucracy (Tucker 94–101; Daniels 82–84).

Laclau and Mouffe deny that this cultural continuity with the czars' feudal regimes explains Stalinism. Laclau and Mouffe argue that the explanation lies in what Leon Trotsky called Russia's "uneven development"—the simultaneous emergence of a feudal peasantry, an industrial working class, Czarist bureaucrats, and other groups belonging to very different historical stages. That is, emerging simultaneously, not in chronological succession, Russia's diverse groups created an anomalous situation in which the frail bourgeoisie could not undertake the modernizing tasks assigned it by established historical schema. These tasks, which included educating and industrializing Soviet society and creating large urban centers and even an independent and democratic civil society, fell instead upon the Russian working class (*Hegemony* 50–54). In other words, since the Soviet communists articulated diverse democratic demands and simultaneous socioeconomic structures, the communists' ideological hegemony, not the fixed, class identity and distinct historical stages of traditional Marxism, explain the Soviet experience.

Some critics object that, in general, Laclau and Mouffe grant hegemonic discourse "an absolute autonomy" or "central role in social and political life" and, as a consequence, "find no alternative short of total contingency, indeterminacy and randomness" (see Larrain 104). Other critics take Laclau's theory to echo the conservative belief that free enterprise has triumphed and that communism as well as Marxism have died; as Terry Eagleton says, the postmodern opposition to traditional Hegelian Marxism "disables radical opponents of the capitalist system just when that system has gotten more powerful than ever" (*Ideology* 381; see also Miklitsch 169 and Žižek, Butler et al. 223). Laclau and Mouffe do consider "the social" an indeterminate or irreducible discourse, rather than a predetermined context or structure, and deny, therefore, the traditional guarantees of a revolutionary social transformation. Laclau rightly maintains, however, that, instead of revolutionary transformation, a radical politics requires strategic argument whose success predetermined working-class or other socioeconomic contexts cannot ensure in advance. He grants that, since contextual oppositions, antagonisms, or exclusions, not essences or transcendent selves, establish identity, the various social movements properly defend their separate interests or their political independence. In *Hegemony*, he and Mouffe argue, however, that the movements also radically extend the Enlightenment tradition of democratic rights. In later work, he maintains that each movement must construct equivalences establishing a hegemonic bloc. Movements should use terms such as "justice" and "equality," which he considers floating signifiers, not universal or transcendent truths, to overcome their local separatism.

Although Simon Critchley, Laclau's colleague at the University of Essex, praises this account of ideological hegemony, he objects that Laclau does not effectively distinguish between normative and ethical forms. Critchley says that, if the normative character of hegemony is merely factual and not ethical, then Laclau has no reason to defend democratic hegemony or to resist ruling-class domination. If the normative character is ethical and not factual, then Laclau's concept of the empty universal is inconsistent because, as Derrida and Heidegger maintain, ethico-ontological ideals require real substance or practical contents, not just arbitrary particulars. As a result, Critchley fears that Laclau's notion of ideological hegemony remains complicit with ruling-class ideology. This fear of complicity implicitly accepts, however, the traditional notion of class conflict and denies or neglects the democratic import of the empty universals, which, by establishing equivalences, can persuade trade unionists, feminists, minorities, and other "new social movements" to form a coalition or hegemonic block.

Other scholars reduce this democratic politics to liberal multiculturalism and defend the antihumanist rationalism of Althusser. For instance, like Laclau and Mouffe, Étienne Balibar, formerly Althusser's colleague and collaborator, repudiates Marxist teleology, construes class struggle as a process, not a social context, acknowledges the assimilation of the working class and the dictatorial character of Marxism, but still considers contradictory relations of exploitation essential to capitalism (see *Race, Nation, Classe* 207–44). More importantly, while Laclau and Mouffe accept the constitutive or persuasive force of discourse, Balibar claims that "genuine" Althusserian theory "takes its distance from any form of 'constructivism' or relativism" (Balibar, "Object" 163). While Laclau and Mouffe accept the independence yet seek to unite the women's, black, or multicultural movements, he condemns not only racist views but all views that grant the autonomy of different races or ethnicities. Echoing American conservatives, he says, for example, that the "dominant theme" of the "new racism" is not "biological heredity but the irreducibility of cultural differences" (33; my translation).

On similar grounds, Alain Badiou, whom Balibar praises for "swimming against the current" of philosophical thought ("History of Truth" 17) repudiates these "multicultural" movements as well as postmodern rhetoric but does not effectively exclude them, totalitarian "evil," or diverse cultural discourses. In *Ethics: An Essay on the Understanding of Evil*, he too supports the antihumanism of Althusser and Foucault but argues that, contrary to Laclau and Mouffe, it undermines liberal ideals of human rights, participatory democracy, and cultural tolerance or inclusion. Of course, he condemns the Nazis' extermination of European Jews and defends the rights of the "sans-papiers" (illegal immigrants); he denies at the same time that political parties, including successful left-wing parties, do much more than represent capital or support the status quo (99).

More importantly, he defends an ethics of truth in which the truths revealed by events disrupt practices of everyday life or undermine scientific forms of knowledge and require reconstruction by the subject as well as his or her fidelity to this reconstruction (see Barker 76). This ethics takes for granted the rationalist notion that mathematics describes reality and the Lacanian notion that, unnameable, reality escapes or resists thought. Since such uncertain or subjective truth becomes a feature of the situation only if the subject succeeds in retrospectively reconstructing or renaming the event, Badiou considers the consistent fidelity to and the militant defense and imposition of this truth the "disinterested" virtue of an immortal self. While Althusser, Foucault, and Laclau and Mouffe repudiate this rationalist faith, Badiou accepts theological ideals in which fidelity counts as grace and the truth, a divine revelation.

Badiou claims that this notion of rationalist ideals and theological truth undercuts multiculturalism, which, he says, makes too much of individual differences or multiplicity (26–27), deconstruction, which presupposes an absolute or divine Other or replaces class struggle with cultural sociology (20–23), and totalitarian "evil," which assumes that the event or situation is full, the simulacrum (what one mistakes for truth) coherent and systematic, and enemies and allies, closed, exclusive sets.

He admits, however, that his account of truth does not effectively exclude rhetoric, opinion, or cultural interests. For example, he considers one's fidelity to the truth revealed by an event a disinterested virtue, but he grants that the simulacrum of truth can also inspire fidelity (74) and that interest and disinterest are readily confused ("[I]t cannot be decided for sure whether the disinterested-interest that animates the becoming-subject of a human animal prevails over interest pure and simple" [78]). He claims that the fidelity inspired by a simulacrum depends on closed nominations such as "Jew" or "blood" and inspires terror, but he grants that the fidelity aroused by truth also "names the adversaries of its perseverance" (75). He complains that, while truth inspires the fidelity of the immortal self, established discourse merely communicates opinion (51–52) but allows that, to overcome totalitarian evil, "at least one real element" of the situation "must be reserved to opinion" because "we must all express our opinions"(85). Jason Barker praises Badiou's defense of truth and opposition to postmodern sophistry, which reduces philosophy, Badiou says, to "conventions, rules, genres of discourse, and plays of language" (cited in Barker 130–31); however, like Balibar's Althusserian science, Badiou's defense of rationalist truth opposes but does not escape such conventions, rules, or plays of language or effectively exclude the rhetoric of cultural interests or values.

Laclau and Mouffe forcefully critique, by contrast, the Hegelian rationalism and theological ideals of traditional Marxism. As Jacob Torfing points out, Laclau's poststructuralist rhetoric, including the notion of hegemonic discourse, the fissured subject, and the empty universal or floating signifier, effectively counters fundamentalist assertions of absolute moral values and essential identities (6). Torfing claims, however, that Laclau and Mouffe "share with Foucault the emphasis on subjectivation, power and politics" (91); actually, Laclau's post-Marxism approximates the messianic Marxism of Jacques Derrida more closely than the disciplinary power or genealogical histories of Foucault.[5] Derrida does not foster a hegemonic bloc of new social movements, yet he too critiques the "onto-theology" of traditional Marxism.

For example, he argues that, in the name of science, Marx condemns the spiritual or spectral other whose recurring phantoms derail the communist movement; however, he fails to exclude this spectral other, whose presence reasserts itself as the revolution's spirit or in other ways (*Specters* 106–109). Derrida maintains that Marx's critique, which includes not only the spirit or specter but also ideology and commodity fetishism, opposes but fails to exclude these spectral others because they are already within Marxism, part of Marx's revolutionary spirit or communist movement. Laclau fears that this logic of the specter can include totalitarian practices, but he accepts this Derridean logic whereby the opposition of flesh and spirit breaks down because the flesh never fully manifests the spirit; as he says, "I have nothing to object to" ("Time" 88).

Derrida goes on to claim, however, that true communism requires a messianic concept of justice. As the "indestructible condition of any deconstruction" and the vital "legacy" of Marx (28), this messianism affirms a transcendent sense of an other, including the dead. Laclau complains that Derrida treats openness to the other as an ethical obligation, not a normative political or hegemonic construct ("Time" 95) but accepts this affirmative messianic Marxism ("Time" 75); however, by undermining "sedimented layers of social practice" and revealing the decisions grounding them, this absolute hospitality to a religious or messianic other always already part of us subverts more than a program of transcendent "onto-theological" truth or purposive "teleo-eschatological" action. In addition, this Derridean messianism resists all established left-wing groups or parties as well. As Zizek says, Derrida's messianic spirit of Marxism renounces "any actual radical political measures" (*Totalitarianism* 154). Similarly, Laclau's post-Marxism dismisses not only Stalinist communism or bureaucratic working-class organizations but all established progressive groups, including trade unions, left-wing political parties, and women's, African American, ethnic, or gay organizations and programs.

In general, Laclau and Mouffe reject not only the Althusserian distinction of science and ideology but also the Foucauldian notion of knowledge and power. Their account of the fissured subject undermines hegemonic assertions of natural values or essential identities but denies the institutional determination of discourse. Laclau and Mouffe argue that theoretical critique resists such institutional conformity and exercises subversive force (*Hegemony* 109). As Anne Smith says, "Against Althusser, then, they would say that . . . we never arrive at a situation in which a ruling force can become so authoritative that it can totally impose its worldview onto the rest of the population" (71). Smith overstates Althusser's "functionalist" view of ruling-class domination but gets Laclau and Mouffe's opposition to his view right: that is, they assume that poststructuralist theory can transcend the divisions and conflicts of modern political discourse and their institutional contexts and expose the antagonisms, dislocations, or fissures which, in Smith's terms, incite "concrete struggles towards progressive social change" (60). As Richard Rorty says, it is Laclau's poststructuralist metalanguage that reveals the antagonisms and conflicts giving the subject his or her fragmented and decentered character (see "Response").

Despite this questionable faith in theoretical critique, Laclau and Mouffe effectively show that hegemonic ideological discourses construct stable but partial or dislocated subjects whose antagonisms or dislocations ensure that they fail to achieve the "full presence" or closure sought by both Marxism and Christianity. Similarly, Judith Butler, whose work I discuss in the next chapter, argues, that, more effectively than Althusser's distinction between science and ideology, a Derridean/psychoanalytic critique of hegemonic domination or interpellation explains the conflicted formation of identity and fosters a democratic politics; she accepts, however, the Foucauldian concept of power/knowledge, which, because it explains the social reproduction of heterosexist norms and identities, justifies feminist and gay movements and groups.

Sex, Gender, and Philosophy

The Feminist Post-Marxism of Judith Butler

It is well known that Judith Butler espouses deconstruction, feminism, psychoanalysis, queer theory, speech-act theory, Foucauldian poststructuralism, Hegelian and Nietzschean philosophy, and so on. Indeed, she adopts so many theories that scholars consider her prose remarkably dense even for an academic. To belittle her prose, Martha Nussbaum says, for example, that, "if you are not familiar with the Althusserian concept of 'interpellation,' you are lost for chapters."[1] Such ridicule assumes that most scholars know remarkably little about and have even less interest in the post-Marxism that she derives not only from Althusser but also from Foucault and Laclau and Mouffe, yet her gay, feminist version of it deepens their theoretical critique and democratic import.

Like them, she critiques the humanist assumption that the subject asserts its individual or prediscursive autonomy and adopts the poststructuralist belief that ideology interpellates and discourses of power/knowledge discipline the subject. As I noted in the last chapter, Laclau and Mouffe repudiate the "functionalism" of Althusser and Foucault; by contrast, Butler claims that both Althusser's notion of interpellation and Foucault's theory of subjugation justify her belief that the heterosexual norms imposed by power govern the construction of gender. While traditional feminists assume that the terms "male" and "female" identify biologically distinct groups with equally distinct interests, experiences, and social organizations, she argues that gender is not a matter of human nature or biological traits but, as Althusser and Foucault imply, a performance imposed by established cultural norms.

Some critics object that this view of gender does not really support agency or resistance because the view denies the subversive force of critique or the normative import of our human nature (see Benhabib and Nussbaum). Other critics say that her view of gender does not foster an oppositional feminist movement, what Amy Allen calls "the kind of power that nourishes collective oppositional social movements such as the feminist movement, and that sustains coalitions between this movement and other social movements" (79). Butler does deny that sexuality is subversive. Like Foucault, who identifies revolutionary politics with the Soviet Gulag, or like Laclau and Mouffe, who reject the distinction between reform and revolution, she takes the heterosexual norms imposed by institutional practices to preclude the political liberation sought by oppositional theorists. In the early *Gender Trouble,* she argues, however, that, by multiplying or parodying the categories of gender, sexuality still fosters resistance or makes gender trouble (34). In other words, as parody or drag, the opposition to gender norms is still practical. In later work, opening these categories to what she calls "rearticulation" or, in Derridean terms, translation by oppressed or excluded groups produces resistance. Moreover, she adopts Hegelian, Nietzschean, and Freudian notions of the unconscious as well as post-Marxist versions of a radical democracy.[2] More radically than antihumanists such as Balibar or Badiou, Slavoj Žižek reduces this democratic ideal to multicultural liberalism and defends traditional Marxist and Stalinist practices on theological grounds. By contrast, although Butler's Hegelian/Nietzchean/Freudian theory contradicts or, as she says, "supplements" the Foucauldian approach, making subjugation the desire of the complicitous subject; her post-Marxist account justifies her performative notion of gender, opening it to articulation by African American, third world, and other peoples of color.

The root of this contradiction is her antihumanist notion that agency is a performance or articulation. As I noted in previous chapters, post-Marxists reject the humanist assumption that the autonomous subject resists its construction or domination by institutional discourses or disciplinary practices. Butler's performative view of gender also rejects the humanist "notion of a voluntarist subject who exists quite apart from the regulatory norms which she/he opposes" (*Bodies* 15) but in a different way. She adopts a Derridean version of John Austin's speech-act theory. Like the later Wittgenstein, who insisted that, in addition to naming or denoting, language involves many sorts of "games," Austin says that some assertions, which he calls constative, describe facts, whereas other assertions, which he calls performative, indicate actions (*How to do Things* 35). Moreover, to explain what makes performative assertions authoritative, he argues that they must meet conventional requirements (89). Butler takes the norms of gender to be performative in this conventional sense; however, just as Derrida claims that Austin's distinction cannot effectively exclude misfires, failures, or literary figures ("Signature" 385–87), so she rejects the constative or referential character of assertions on the grounds that constative assertions require policing to suppress abnormalities. As she says, "[T]he constative claim (about sex) is always to some degree performative (of gender)" (*Bodies* 11). In Derridean terms, Butler argues that, "as a reiterative or rearticulatory practice," agency is "immanent to power, and not a relation of external opposition to power" (*Bodies* 15). That is, because descriptive or constative assertions are always performative as well, she considers agency only "a reiterative or rearticulatory practice" situated within or "immanent to power."

In addition, in the Althusserian manner Butler roots this performative view of gender in material or institutional practices. As I explained in chapters 1 and 2, Althusser claims that, constituting or interprellating the subject, ideology is rooted in institutional rituals that reproduce it; similarly, Foucault suggests that, opposed to the ruling classes' unifying intentions, the discourses of power/knowledge impose normality and thereby reproduce themselves and/or the subject. Unlike Laclau and Mouffe, who consider this Althusserian "logic of reproduction" functionalist, Butler brings together speech-act theory and ideological reproduction. For instance, in *Excitable Speech*, she claims that

> Austin's view that the illocutionary speech act is conditioned by its conventional, that is, "ritual" or "ceremonial" dimension, finds a counterpart in Althusser's insistence that ideology has a "ritual" form, and that ritual constitutes "the material existence of an ideological apparatus" (168). Ritual is material to the extent that it is productive, that is, it produces the belief that appears to be "behind" it. (24–25)

Rooted in the state's social institutions or "ideological apparatus," these material rituals justify Butler's claim that, far from ensuring the subject's autonomy, agency rearticulates and gender performs authoritative conventions.

Consider, for example, her critique of Simone de Beauvoir's existential humanism. In *The Second Sex*, de Beauvoir maintains that the masculine is constructed as a disembodied universal, while the feminine is depicted as a subjective particular. She says that men can base their views on their objectivity because they believe that they relate directly to nature, whereas, related to the body, the views of women are taken to express their sex, rather than their objectivity.

She claims, moreover, that women can attain freedom only if, like men, they assert their subjectivity and attain transcendence. To summarize briefly her rich historical perspective, she shows that in nomadic hunting and gathering societies, women, confined to domestic duties, were trapped in immanence, whereas men, who hunted or fished for food, conquered nature and attained transcendence. When agricultural societies developed, women remained trapped in immanence, so men were able to subjugate them, making them the vehicle of their newly established private property. In subsequent eras, the laws, religions, customs, literature, and art confirmed this state of immanence or granted women independence if the men desired it. Only in the modern industrial era, when women can acquire a profession, education, rights, and contraceptive devices, have they attained freedom.

In *Gender Trouble*, Butler does not examine the changing historical configurations of women's social contexts and cultural ideals; however, she admits de Beauvoir's claim that a disembodied universality characterizes the masculine gender, while a subjective particularity describes the feminine; she denies, however, that women will win their freedom if they assert their subjectivity and attain transcendence. She fears that this claim presupposes the legitimacy of the humanist notion that the mind and body form a dualism (10). Butler is right: de Beauvoir maintains that, unlike the women who lived in past eras, "the modern woman" has the power to resist gender differences and achieve transcendence because these notions implicitly accept the traditional humanist distinction between the limited, subjective body and the infinite, universal soul.

Stella Sandford objects, however, that de Beauvoir does not adopt a humanist or Cartesian dualism of body and mind; de Beauvoir accepts the nonessentialist, existential belief that human being is constituted by human action. Sandford points out that de Beauvoir's famous distinction between sex, which is biological, and gender, which is cultural or artificial, shows this existential appreciation of action; in de Beauvoir's terms, "One is not born, but rather becomes, a woman" (267). In *Gender Trouble* Butler grants that one becomes a woman as de Beauvoir says, but rejects the distinction of sex and gender on the grounds that both of them are performative or culturally constructed (8). Butler claims not only that the norms of gender do not derive from one's physical nature; in addition, they impose a performance constructing the body as male or female (*Gender Trouble* 22–23). In other words, neither an autonomous subject nor an objective body can determine one's sex and gender; rather, they are both constituted by the norms stipulating what one's gender is. These norms purport to describe one's sex and gender but actually impose them (24–25).

Critics object that to dismiss de Beauvoir's existentialist notion of being or ontology and make both sex and gender performative is to lapse into the idealist belief that discourse constitutes being (see Sandford and Rothenberg and Valente). As Toril Moi says, "[E]ven if language and discourse were material" in Butler's Althusserian sense, "they surely would not be material in quite the same way as educational institutions, women's wages, women's legal and political status, or women's access to contraception and abortion."[3] If the conventions governing the performance of gender have a genuinely "material existence" in an "ideological apparatus," as Butler claims, this distinction between language and discourse, on the one hand, and "educational institutions, women's wages, women's legal and political status, or women's access to contraception and abortion," on the other, breaks down.

The trouble is not that Butler fails to distinguish these types of material existence but that she does not consistently accept the "material existence" of the institutional rituals that, according to Althusser and Foucault, reproduce conventions. Although she grants, for example, that authoritative ideologies interpellate or "hail" the subject, as Althusser argues, she still complains that he adopts a theological notion of voice which the subject finds "almost impossible to refuse" because of his or her "original guilt" (*Psychic* 109–110). Similarly, even though Foucault rightly shows, she says, that the "matrices of power and discourse that constitute the subject are neither singular nor sovereign" (*Psychic* 5), she objects that his account also does not explain why individuals subjugate themselves to power. For instance, in *The Psychic Life of Power*, she says that he fails to grasp the full nature of subjugation, which explains the desire moving the subject to accept his or her subjugation or the desire compelling the victim to preserve his or her identity as victim. As she says, "The Foucaultian postulation of subjection assumes a specific psychoanalytic valence when we consider that no subject emerges without a passionate attachment to those on whom he or she is fundamentally dependent" (*Psychic* 7; see also *Contingencies* 151). Although Foucault claims that, far from transforming the institutional practices constructing subjectivity, Freudian theory articulates them, Butler maintains that that theory exposes the complicity of the subject, revealing his or her "passionate attachment to those on whom he or she is fundamentally dependent." Foucault rejects Hegelian theory, but she defends it on similar grounds: Hegel's account of the "unhappy conscience" shows that the bondsman achieves independence of the lord only by imposing the lord's ideals on himself. Nietzsche too, she claims, believes that the subject's desire for power explains why it adopts the norms and ideals of power and thereby subjugates itself.

Moving beyond her antihumanist poststructuralism, this Hegelian/Nietschean/Freudian account of subjugation and complicity creates an inconsistency, what Seyla Benhabib terms a "fissure between psychoanalytic theory and Foucauldianism" (120). As I noted, Butler adopts the Foucauldian notion that, as performative, the norms of gender render agency as the effect of power, not as the subject's independent choice; nonetheless, to preserve theoretical critique, she accepts as well the incompatible Hegelian/Nietzschean/Derridean/Freudian theory, which claims that the subject enslaves itself because of its desire for power. Moreover, this theory maintains that the exclusions or limitations imposed by an assertion or action always come back to undermine or dissolve it, what she calls "the disruptive return of the excluded from within the very logic of the heterosexual symbolic" (*Bodies* 212–18).[4] Implicitly reinstating the totality, this return of the repressed "exclusions or limitations" preserves Hegelian theoretical self-consciousness but not Foucault's poststructuralism, which, as I noted, shows that such an implicitly totalizing account cannot overcome a discourse's divisions or oppositions because they are rooted in the history or genealogy of authoritative practices.

Rosemary Hennessy complains that, because of Butler's Foucauldian poststructuralism, Butler dismisses historical analysis in favor of theoretical critique. As Hennessy says, while Butler wrongly "displaces analysis of social totalities like capitalism and patriarchy . . . in favor of an exclusive emphasis on the specific and the social (à la Foucault)," a genuine "historicizing" acknowledges that "the continuation of social life depends on its (re)production in various spheres" (150). This objection mistakenly assumes that only totalizing Hegelian or Marxist theory describes a discourse's conflicts, development, or reproduction, whereas, like Foucault, who indicates how established discourses of punishment, sexuality, money, or madness reproduce and develop themselves, Butler shows that the material rituals of the ideological apparatus reproduce such discourses. Hennessy rightly suggests, however, that Butler dismisses the historical study of the divisions and conflicts informing established discourses and instead engages in a theoretical critique of their exclusions and repressions.

Other critics find Butler's performative view of gender paradoxical, rather than contradictory, because they consider her view both oppositional and determinist.[5] In the antihumanist fashion, Butler argues that "the agency denoted by the performativity of 'sex' will be directly counter to any notion of a voluntarist subject who exists quite apart from the regulatory norms which she/he opposes"; however, since the reiteration or rearticulation of gender voices the unconscious or the disunity of the subject, Butler also claims that reiteration enables the subject to resist the normalization imposed by Foucauldian notions of power. As I already suggested, this account of individual refusal or resistance inconsistently denies Foucault's belief that institutional practices, rather than theoretical ideals, reproduce the subject. Moreover, to establish feminist, gay, or Marxist discourses in an institutional context successfully is to impose a positive or progressive normalization; whereas, like Laclau's

Derridean theory, which dismisses the reproduction of both progressive and conservative discourses, Butler's revision of Foucault opposes all normalization, progressive or not: as she says, "Must the social always be equated with the given and the normalizable?" (102).

Critics also object that Butler's performative notion of identity lacks the normative foundations provided by Habermas's concept of rational communication or Aristotle's notion of human nature (see Benhabib and Nussbaum). I grant that her Derridean/Hegelian defense of psychoanalytic theory contradicts her Althusserian/Foucauldian account of gender as performance, leaving her account of the complicitous subject who subjugates itself unable to distinguish between a progressive and reactionary normalization of power. On the other hand, construing agency or resistance "as a reiterative or rearticulatory practice, immanent to power" allows Butler to engage Laclau's notion of hegemony, whose feminist, minority, third world, gay, and working-class "rearticulations" one cannot stipulate in advance or regulate in keeping with some established norm.[6]

In *Bodies That Matter*, for example, she claims that rearticulation endows what Laclau terms the empty universals of democratic politics with feminist, minority, or working-class substance, but she reformulates this view in Lacanian terms, according to which "political signifiers" such as "women," "democracy," or "freedom" are "empty signs which come to bear phantasmic investments of various kinds" (*Bodies* 191). Laclau claims, however, that, like a rock, Lacan's concept of the real, not Foucauldian or poststructuralist notions of discourse, explains the subject's "phantasmic investments" in political signifiers. Butler objects that this notion of the real treats the incest taboo and its heterosexist ideals as a universal truth, rather than as a cultural norm, but she still accepts Laclau's critique of traditional Marxism. That is, hegemonic ideology, not ruling-class interests, explains the formation of the subject's identity, and the endless antagonisms of the subject's groups and movements, not the conflicting interests of opposed classes, explain the limits or incompleteness of this identity (see *Contingency* 29).

In *Contingency, Hegemony, Universality*, she goes on to reject Laclau's notion of empty universals in favor of the Derridean practice of cultural translation. What she argues is that Laclau's notion of empty universals takes for granted the Kantian belief that the schema of rationality or universality transcend the particular contexts of culture or social life. Just as the Lacanian notion of the real divorces the incest taboo from its legitimating cultural contexts, so too this notion of empty universals reifies the structures justifying them. As a result, this notion isolates them from the contexts legitimating them and excluding contrary claims. Butler points out, for example, that, if gay couples win the right to marry and form a family, they obtain a justifying universality but exclude other sorts of relationships, including "single mothers or single fathers, people who are divorced, people who are in relationships that are not marital in kind or status, other lesbian, gay, and transgender people whose sexual relations are multiple" (*Contingency* 176).

While Laclau defends such exclusions and, as a result, divorces the universal and the particular, the cultural translation that Butler derives from Gayatri Spivak preserves the intimate relationship of the two. As Butler says,

> And what emerges is a kind of political claim which, I would argue, is neither exclusively universal nor exclusively particular; where, indeed, the particular interests that inhere in certain cultural formulations of universality are exposed, and no universal is freed from its contamination by the particular contexts from which it emerges and in which it travels. (40)

Since "the universal does not escape contamination by the particular contexts from which it emerges," Butler claims that this cultural translation negotiates incompatible or competing universalities in a historical way, rather than in what she terms Laclau's reified manner.

Laclau grants that particulars contaminate universals, as Butler says, but he argues that every approach makes formal or systematic claims justifying its methods. As he says, Butler never explains how she defines "the conditions of context-dependency and historicity as such" (Butler et al. 183). Laclau is right: in a Hegelian manner Butler treats universal claims as though they were a feature of a particular context and not a construct of her discourse; nonetheless, her Derridean notion of cultural translation is democratic because it opens modernity's key terms—human rights, justice—to articulation by groups whom the Eurocentric or heterosexual biases of modernity exclude. As a result, even though her performative view of gender makes the subject complicit in his or her own domination, her reconstruction of gender differences as hegemonic ideology effectively extends her view of gender to multicultural articulations or translations.

Slavoj Zizek also accepts Laclau and Mouffe's claim that hegemonic ideological formations construct a fissured identity and that "empty universals" explain the subject's "phantasmic investments" in political signifiers; however, Zizek rejects Butler's belief that her performative view of gender opens the articulation of empty signifiers like "equality" or "independence" to excluded multicultural groups. More radically than Balibar and Badiou, Zizek reduces this multicultural politics to a "disinvolved, inverted, self-referential" form of racism and vindicates traditional Marxism, including its Stalinist versions.[7]

In a Hegelian fashion, Zizek assumes that only a "privileged universal position" overcomes racism or respects the Other's identity or community. As a result, he considers multiculturalism the other side of the "world capitalist system" ("And, of course, the ideal form of ideology of this global capitalism is multiculturalism" [*Ticklish* 216]) and faults its complicity. As he says, while "we are fighting our PC battles for the rights of ethnic minorities, of gays and lesbians, of different lifestyles, and so forth, . . . today's critical theory, in the guise of 'cultural studies,' is performing the ultimate service for the unrestrained development of capitalism by actively participating in the ideological effort to render its massive presence invisible" (*Ticklish* 218).

Like Butler, Zizek accepts as well Althusser's theory of ideological interpellation. He maintains, for example, that "it is precisely because 'class struggle' interpellates individuals to adopt the subjective stance of a 'proletarian' that its appeal is universal."[8] Zizek argues, however, that Badiou's notion of fidelity turns Althusser's theory around, making grace and revelation, not science, the grounds of a truth-event (*Ticklish* 145). Since one who is interpellated as a proletarian subject "recognizes himself in the call of the Truth-event" or is "touched by grace" (*Ticklish* 217), Zizek treats Marxist notions of class struggle and the capitalist system as a matter of faith, not reason. "What if . . . the true fidelity to the Event is 'dogmatic' in the precise sense of unconditional Faith[?]" (*Ticklish* 144).

Butler adopts Laclau and Mouffe's skeptical notion of hegemony because "democracy is secured precisely through its resistance" to these traditional Marxist ideas (Butler et al. 268). Moreover, she faults those "Marxist states" that took Marx's ideas to justify central regulation and control and undemocratic practices, whereas Zizek defends Stalinist Marxism. For instance, he argues that, contrary to totalitarian theory as well as neo-liberalism, Stalinist and Nazi practices do not parallel each other. The paradoxes of the confessed revolutionary—guilty because he was loyal and devoted—give Stalinism a religious character foreign to Nazism, which found no value in Jewish confessions (*Ticklish* 227; see also *Did Somebody Say* 100–101). He maintains, in addition, that Stalin did not initiate a reign of terror in order to impose his tyrannical rule, as totalitarian theorists claim; the Stalinist terror developed because the rule of the Communist Party broke down. Like Mao, who, to reform the party, initiated the youthful Red Guard, Stalin set the elite *nomenklatura* of the Party against its rank and file and, as a result, lost control of the Party apparatus.

Zizek forcefully critiques these parallels between Stalinism and Nazism, but, like him, totalitarian theorists say that Stalin acquired a divine infallibility entirely compatible with those oppositional tactics but foreign to liberal democracy. They too consider Marxist theory a religious dogma whose violence and tyranny Stalinism revealed. Zizek complains that Balibar and Badiou accept a "marginalist politics" in which their political failure preserves their theoretical authenticity (*Ticklish* 232–33), but his theological defense of Marxist theory also emphasizes the authenticity of its traditional notions. By contrast, like Laclau and Mouffe, Butler adopts a skeptical, Derridean notion of cultural articulation or translation which opens modernity's key terms—human rights, justice—to independent articulation by feminist, minority, third world, gay, and working-class groups. Moreover, as I indicate in the next two chapters, the skeptical Foucauldian or materialist aesthetics of Pierre Macherey and the cultural theory of Tony Bennett, John Frow, and Toby Miller also allow such radical translation, rearticulation, or reception of aesthetic or cultural values; however, while Butler's Freudian/Hegelian/Nietzschean defense of psychoanalytic theory makes the subject complicit in his or her own domination, Macherey and Bennett consistently repudiate Butler's and Laclau's faith in theoretical critique and produce profound histories of literary and philosophical movements.

From Althusserian Science to Foucauldian Materialism

The Later Work of Pierre Macherey

In 1988, when I visited Pierre Macherey in his Parisian apartment, he sat quietly in a big lounge chair surrounded by shelves of books while I gradually summarized several British and American critiques of his famous *A Theory of Literary Production* (1966). After fifteen minutes, he abruptly exclaimed, "I wrote that book over twenty years ago," and, running around the room, gathered reprints of his recent essays and handed them to me.

His dismissive reaction was appropriate. In the earlier work, Macherey, who was Althusser's student, colleague, and collaborator for more than ten years, defends the Althusserian belief that scientific Marxism opposes Stalinist and humanist theory and that literature, situated between science and ideology, shows but does not tell the truth. Like Foucault, Laclau and Mouffe, Butler, and, to an extent, Althusser himself, Macherey goes on in later work to repudiate the Althusserian opposition of science and ideology as well as the disciplinary divisions of literature and philosophy. As I indicated in previous chapters, Althusser preserves a particular science's formal independence of its ideology, but he and Foucault examine the sociohistorical "problematic" or "archaeology" of particular sciences, disciplines, or discourses. Repudiating such historical determination as functionalist, Laclau and Mouffe and, to an extent, Butler foster the democratizing articulations or translations of the women's, black, postcolonial, or other contemporary social movements. Inspired by Michel Foucault's archealogical studies, Macherey shows, by contrast, that, far from grounding positive or scientific knowledge or enabling resistance, theory is always situated in a practical context in which it reveals the antagonisms of and takes a position on the contrary views forming the context. Moreover, Macherey, who grants the validity of a work's misreadings, what he calls "true errors," evaluates a work's historical influence and philosophy's institutional contexts.

The Althusserian Work

In his influential early work, he defends Althusser's claim that Marx breaks with humanism and establishes a scientific Marxism. For example, in "One divides into Two," which Althusser urged Macherey to publish, he complains that humanism denies the reality of contradiction and, as a result, sets the unified character of humanity above the class struggle (*Histoires* 66–68). In "A Propos de la Rupture" (1965), he argues that science, which is conceptual knowledge, opposes the humanist ideology and that, properly interpreted, Marx's work reveals a rupture between them.

Althusser assigned Macherey the task of developing the literary import of this Althusserian perspective (See Montag, *Althusser* 49–50). In *A Theory* Macherey does so, arguing that, like Marxist science, literary criticism that rigorously defines its object, carefully limits its field, and vigorously demystifies ideology attains the status of a genuine science. That is, situated between objective science and humanist ideology, literature reworks ideological discourses but docs not know or denote them. Literature produces new outlooks and contexts, parodies and deforms ideology, exposing its limits and gaps, but does not recognize or condemn it. Macherey adds that the ordinary reader falls victim to ideology, whose hidden purposes he inadvertently carries out, but the scientific critic discovers the ideological import of the gaps created by literary production because the critic has objective knowledge of history (1–14).

Writing at the same time, Roland Barthes also claimed that criticism becomes science, but in the structuralist manner he argued that writing provides the "object-language" for which structuralism represents a "meta-language." Macherey also assumes that the critic's scientific language or discourse matters, but Macherey says that what gives the work its insight into history is the productive activity of the author, not his or her beliefs. For example, Macherey shows that in *A Journey to the Center of the Earth* Jules Verne depicts the adventures of an engineer, whose constant hurry conveys an industrial society's sense of time and of purpose and whose adventures and discoveries justify the bourgeois belief that science and technology enable humanity to master nature and colonize the world. At the same time, Verne reworks the story of Robinson Crusoe, whose lonely isolation on a mysterious island anticipates and undermines such discovery and conquest. In Verne's version, a group of explorers, not a solitary individual, discovers a mysterious isle within the earth, but Captain Nemo, the mysterious occupant of the isle, precedes them and exposes their moral faults. Macherey grants that Verne recognized the limits of his era's scientific outlook, but Macherey argues that Verne's text still betrays an irreconcilable conflict between industrial science's domination and humanity's moral limits.

As this conflict of industry and morality suggests, Macherey assumes that Verne's productive activity, not his or her intentions or beliefs, explains the novel's insights into historical reality. To an extent, this notion of literary productivity takes for granted the traditional formal belief that, even though the empirical text reveals gaps and inconsistencies, the ideal text forms a unified whole. This notion also accepts the phenomenological belief that, while a text realizes a writer's intentions, its gaps and inconsistencies stimulate the reader's activity (see Moyra Hazlett 70–71). Formal textual criticism maintains, however, that the reader's activity does not determine the text's meaning, which is objective, and phenomenological criticism assumes that, even though the text's gaps stimulates the reader's activity, the text still governs what the reader does. By contrast, Macherey sharply distinguishes the conditions in which the writer produces a work from those in which the reader receives it. For instance, he analyzes the classic detective story from two perspectives—the spatial and the temporal. Temporally, the crimes in the story make no sense until a sleuth like Sherlock Holmes explains them; they are irrational until the hero-detective uncovers their rationality. In other words, to achieve closure, the story requires the reader to proceed chronologically, the experience of the crimes coming before the explanation of their solution. This temporal approach is different from the spatial perspective, in which the artist produces both the irrationality making the crime a puzzle and the rationality making it perfectly clear. The story must create contrary effects: the crime should seem both inexplicable and well-explained, mysterious and sensible (*Theory* 18–19). To produce these opposed effects, the artist follows a spatial strategy in which the mystery and the explanation coexist and do not precede each other. Ideology still traps the unscientific reader, but Macherey shows that artistic production follows conventions, rules, and relationships quite distinct from those of artistic reception.

The Foucauldian Work

Similarly, in "Literature as an Ideological Form: Some Marxist Propositions" (1981), Macherey and Balibar consider the romantic identification of the reader with the author's perspective or social context misleading; the readers' various reproductions of the work may include significant deviations from the author's perspective. The reader gains greater independence, for the productive activity of the work now includes the new contexts and conventions in terms of which subsequent readers reproduce literature or philosophy. The absences, gaps, and inconsistencies of a work still betray its conditions of production, but they include diverse philosophies, their influential proponents, the acceptable literary forms, and the education and social ties of writers and readers.

Macherey and Balibar still maintain that the critical insights produced by literature reflect reality but the reality reflected by it is the institutional world of discourses, forms, and conventions, not the objective truths of positive science nor the partial truths of a manipulative ideology. Like Foucault, by whose notion of an episteme Macherey was, he says, "particularly stimulated" (See *dinosaure* 167–68), he goes on to explain the diverse ways in which the works of George Sand, George Bataille, Gustave Flaubert, the marquis de Sade, or Victor Hugo elaborate a period's archive of conventions and norms. For example, Macherey says that Hugo's *Les Misérables* describes society as a sea in which, like the night, uncertain characters appear and disappear (*Object* 91). He claims that this description takes for granted an episteme in which a subterranean man emerges from a tumultuous society. Created by the press and elaborated from 1840 to 1850, this episteme informs the work of the radical Karl Marx, the conservative Alexis de Tocqueville, as well as liberal social theorists; however, unlike Jules Verne's apologetic account of industrial society's origins, this episteme does not represent an ideological project. Macherey admits that French society ultimately grants the man below a structural position, that, as a result, this episteme governs French social relations in this era, but not that the episteme, or mythology, improves or distorts the era's understanding of social change. He recognizes that, to explain society's conditions of existence, a great period of history elaborates such an episteme, yet, like Foucault, he considers it a functional necessity, not the improved understanding nor the distorted representation required by the familiar Marxist opposition of science/ideology.

Althusser also criticizes the broad opposition of science and ideology and examines a discourse or discipline's historical context of conventions and practices, what he calls its "problematic." In the early *For Marx*, he defended the rationalist faith that rigorous conceptual analysis enables theory to resist ideological interpellation and effectively grasp the universal truths of experience. In later works, he rejects such foundational theory, which he terms "theoreticism"; as he says, Marx repudiated "every philosophical ideology of the subject" because it "gave classical bourgeois philosophy the means of *guaranteeing* its ideas, practices, and goals" (*Essays* 178).

Macherey also repudiates "foundational" theory but in a different way. Like the neopragmatist Richard Rorty, who rejects the foundational norms dividing literature and philosophy,[1] he challenges literature's and philosophy's disciplinary boundaries; as he says, "[T]he encounter which constitutes Literature and Philosophy as autonomous essences confined to the respective fields which define them and establish their limits, is a product of history. . . . Could the moment of that division have passed?" (*Object* 4–5). Not only does he repudiate the historical divisions consigning philosophy and literature to "essentialist" disciplines, he also rejects the "foundational" assumptions whereby philosophy appropriates the right to speak the truth about literature and literature presents itself as the repressed other or concealed truth of philosophy. Neither philosophy nor literature possesses the ultimate truth; rather, the production of the text weaves the two together, producing a unique insight which is both and neither.

Macherey repudiates foundational theory as well as the science/ideology opposition but he claims that the work's realizations in new contexts produce new insights. Far from establishing positive or scientific knowledge, these new realizations involve misinterpretations and misunderstandings, which, in turn, constitute the work's rich history. What, as I noted in the previous chapters, Laclau and Butler call articulations or translations Macherey terms misreadings or "true errors": in his terms, "what at first regard appear to be of the order of falsification, concerted or involuntary, returns in forms of expression which, for being deviants, are not less authentic in their manner and in any case necessary" (*dinosaure* 173; my translation). As "true errors," these "forms of expression" open the history of a text to its readers' conventions, ideologies, and beliefs, what literary critics such as Tony Bennett term its reception.

Consider, for example, Macherey's different accounts of Spinoza's philosophy. In the Althusserian *Hegel ou Spinoza* (1979), Macherey says that Spinoza's material concept of substance is more truthful than Hegel's notion of Spirit because Spinoza's concept of substance acts in diverse modes and does not mediate contradictory moments, whereas the self-conscious Spirit of Hegel denies the ambiguity of historical developments and favors a teleological kind of evolution. In the Foucauldian *dinosaure*, Macherey is particularly interested in Hegel's misreadings of Spinoza, not in who is right. For instance, he points out that "[t]he Spinoza of the *Science of Logic*, a primitive, oriental theorist of indeterminate being, is not at all that of the *Lessons of the History of Philosophy* . . . essentially a postCartesian philosopher, a 'modern,' marked by the categories of reflection and analysis of what Hegel calls a logic of essence" (*dinosaure* 174). These different versions of Spinoza are not mistaken; they show how Hegel elaborated his system.

In the Althusserian work, the critic who possesses a science of ideologies overcomes the influence of these conventions, ideologies, and beliefs, and, unlike ordinary readers, who remain enthralled to them, grasps the work's unstated insight into historical reality. Thus, in *A Journey* Verne's productive activity moves the text beyond Verne's belief that his era's scientific outlook is limited, revealing thereby what ordinary readers miss—an irreconcilable conflict between industrial science's domination and humanity's moral limits. In the Foucauldian work, the critic still evaluates a work's insights but does not consider the views of ordinary readers blindly ideological or tell them why they should value the work or what its real virtue is; rather, he or she explains what influence it has exerted or how they have construed the work and why. Macherey claims, moreover, that what such true misconstruals indicate is that, contrary to Marx, philosophy is not "merely a factitious, inactive reflection, powerless to act upon things, able only to speak about them while leaving them unchanged" ("[L]a philosophie n'est pas . . . ce reflet factice et inactive, impuissant à agir sur des choses qu'il ne ferait que représenter en les laissant comme elles sont") (*dinosaure* 91). Because of the diverse realizations, misinterpretations, and misunderstandings, philosophy has its own history.

Terry Eagleton also produces and subsequently repudiates an Althusserian account of literary criticism, but he defends the subversive import of humanist aesthetics, not this Foucauldian notion of rich misreadings. In *Criticism and Ideology* (1976), which was influenced by Macherey, Eagleton claims that literary texts rework the signs of ideology, exposing their gaps, speaking their silences. Eagleton also expects Marxist science to overcome the biases of cultural institutions and reveal the text's insight into history. He grants that the objective values of the text do not erase the influence of authors or readers and that neither the established canon nor the critical tradition ensures that the critic transcends his subjectivity. He argues, nonetheless, that the critic who possesses a science of ideologies escapes their influence, transcends his own arbitrariness, and perceives the reader's, the text's, and history's "true" relationships (*Criticism* 96).

In the 1980s, when the poststructuralist era begins, Eagleton confesses that the scientific formalism of *Criticism and Ideology* is "elitist" and, like Macherey, Laclau and Mouffe, and, as I will shortly show, Bennett and Frow, abandons it. Eagleton goes on, however, to defend the progressive import of liberal humanism, whose notion of aesthetics, despite its "specious form of universality," envisions "human energies as radical ends in themselves which is the implacable enemy of all dominative or instrumentalist thought" (*The Ideology of the Aesthetic* 9) and to debunk the work of Foucault, whose notion of the body acts "among other things as a convenient displacement of a less immediately corporeal politics, and . . . as an ersatz kind of ethics" (*The Ideology of the Aesthetic* 7). Moreover, he lampoons the radical pretensions of what he derisively labels the "readers' liberation movement"("The Revolt" 449–52).

Macherey also repudiates the scientific criticism of his Althusserian work, but, consistently opposing foundational humanist notions of theoretical autonomy or opposition, he claims that what explains a work's public import is a Foucauldian history of its realizations, misreadings, or influence. Instead of defending the capacity of aesthetics or theory to resist "all dominative or instrumentalist thought," he argues that a materialist philosophy takes a position in a practical context in which positive knowledge or theories reveal the oppositions that determine the context. As I noted, in *Reading Capital*, Althusser also repudiates the autonomous norms of theory, and, even though he preserves the opposition of science and ideology, he develops a Foucauldian notion of a science's or discourse's "knowledge effect." In addition, he justifies a partisan stance in philosophical contexts but construes this partisanship in Marxist terms, as a subjective or "relativist" commitment to the class struggle.

Macherey also defends such partisanship but denies that the notion of class struggle or the opposition of idealism/materialism adequately explains it. In "In a materialist way" (1983), he faults Marx and Engel's critique of Hegel's idealist dialectics, which claims that adverse or opposite theories confront each other in a conflictual manner. He grants that the "materialist" core of Hegel's dialectic is, as they claimed, "'wrapped' in a teleological discourse of a unitary nature affirming the ineluctable reconciliation of these opposites" (141). He maintains, however, that they got his idealism wrong: as Macherey says, "Their blunder corresponds precisely to the illusion of an independent theoretical knowledge, realized in the form of a doctrinaire materialism" (141). Reducing such theoretical knowledge to a "blunder," Macherey, like Althusser and Laclau and Mouffe, repudiates the "doctrinaire materialism" of a Marx or a Lenin as well as the speculative humanism of a Hegel or an Adorno. The history of philosophy still includes diverse and contrary systems in contradiction with each other, as Hegel claimed, but a materialist philosophy does

not construct positive knowledge revealing their underlying social context or a purely theoretical truth resisting
or transcending "instrumental reason"; rather, taking a
stand, this philosophy explains and evaluates their oppositions, contexts, and motivations in sociohistorical but not
in class terms.

For instance, far from condemning the humanism of
Madame de Staël, he shows that she imposed on the French
the "creative" belief that Immanuel Kant reconciles senti-
ment and reflection and, thereby, defends an obscure, formal, but still vital kind of "philosophical enthusiasm" (*Object*
28–29). He also shows that she created an original and influential view of German culture, according to which the "en-
thusiastic" philosophical spirit of the Germans forcefully
reconciles the heart and the mind, or the universal concept
and the concrete reality, but the fragmented character of the
German nation isolates the Germans, rendering them abstract, sectarian, and impractical (*Object* 30–35). He grants
that de Staël disseminated the ideas of Montesquieu,
Herder, and Möser but maintains that neither the truth of
these ideas nor her conscious beliefs about them explain the
import of her work; rather, because she was situated at the
borders where German, French, and other cultures meet,
she was able to create an influential mythology which
described Germans as idealist dreamers asleep in a spiritual
fog and which "dominated France for more than half a century" (*Object* 30).

On these historical grounds, he appreciates not only the
humanism of Madame de Staël but also that of George Sand,
who interpreted G. W. F. Hegel's theories as a religion of humanity, as well as the antihumanism of Raymond Roussel,
whose linguistic constructions achieved the scientific imper-
sonality of Ferdinand de Saussure, Sigmund Freud, and
even Martin Heidegger. In a similar way he shows that some
writers, including Flaubert and Sade, digest all things in
order to restore them in what Macherey calls a "dematerial-
ized form" (*Object* 235). Other writers, including Roussel,
Celine, or Mallarmé, emphasize style in order to describe
what Macherey considers a world devastated by words and

events (*Object* 237). Macherey insists that these writers matter because their productive activity effectively undermined established metaphysical justifications of reality.

In addition, Macherey points out that Alexander Kojève, who interpreted Hegelian theory as an account of posthistorical modernity, taught George Bataille, André Breton, Jacques Lacan, Raymond Queneau, and other important French artists and intellectuals to appreciate Hegelian language (*Object* 59–60). He cannot understand how they could accept Kojève's belief that history has come to an end (*Object* 67–68), but he still describes the extensive influence of Kojève's Hegel. Similarly, Macherey says that Bataille's belief in a divided human essence missing to itself influences Lacan's account of the unconscious (*Object* 129), while Bataille's materializing materialism, which inverts traditional values in a Nietzschean way, influences Foucault.

In the Althusserian *A Theory*, Macherey claims that Verne's *A Journey to the Center of the Earth* is a valuable novel because, despite Verne's beliefs, his productive activity reveals an irreconcilable conflict between science's domination and humanity's moral limits. In these Foucauldian studies, Macherey still evaluates a writer's productive activity, but he suggests that the productive activity of writers and readers is valuable not because they produce scientific insights into historical reality but because they influence their sociohistorical contexts. Hence, far from opposing her humanist ideology or revealing the scientific truth, Macherey appreciates the extensive influence that Madame de Staël's humanist views of Kant and Germans exerted in nineteenth-century France.

Warren Montag says that, far from rejecting Althusserian Marxism, Macherey simply tries to "discover new points of application" from which he could speak about its "problems and questions" more effectively ("Introduction" 13); however, this notion of material influence or partisanship sharply divides scientific and poststructuralist Althusserians. For instance, Étienne Balibar, who preserves the conceptual truth of Althusserian theory, dismisses such partisanship. Mixing up taking a stand and imitating reality, he claims that such partisanship implies that the "concept of a dog (a barking animal) must itself bark" (*Écrit* 81) and goes on to dismiss "any form of 'constructivism' or relativism, even in the sophisticated form given it by Foucault" (Balibar, "Object" 163; see also Nelson, 166–67; Resch 166; Smith, *Reading* 81–82, and 215; Sprinker, "Current Conjuncture" 829–31). Moreover, Balibar labels Althusser's critique of his earlier theoreticism suicidal and his political situation schizophrenic, thereby implying that Althusser's self-criticism and theoretical partisanship and his nightmarish murder of his wife Hélène Rytman are similar ("Structural" 111). By contrast, Resnick and Wolff defend Althusser's critique of his earlier theoreticism, which, they say, parallels Richard Rorty's poststructuralist critique (*Knowledge* 17–19, 94–95). Moreover, they claim that, on the basis of an existing theory's conditions and consequences, a Marxian epistemology judges the theory's acceptability or adopts a partisan attitude toward it ("Althusser's Liberation" 67); as they say, Marxian theory's "'relativist' commitment to the plurality of theories and their truths is merely the prelude for the specification of their partisan positions" (*Knowledge* 36).

Macherey does not say that a "Marxian" method characterizes theories as a plurality; rather, his Foucaultian materialism situates positive knowledge or theories in the practical, discursive context in which they reveal the oppositions determining the context. He too claims, however, that this approach adopts a partisan position: it evaluates a work's public import or influence, which, as I noted, stem from the writer's and the reader's productive activity.

As a result, Macherey's Foucauldian materialism achieves great historical depth. Critics object, however, that, by rejecting scientific Marxism, such "postmodern" approaches accommodate the dominant liberalism.[2] It is true that in a postmodern fashion both Macherey and Rorty, a liberal neopragmatist, reject the foundational norms of literature and philosophy. Macherey and Rorty both wish to merge philosophy and literature, but Rorty, who defends the traditional, liberal distinction between public and private realms, dismisses Foucault on the grounds that "[t]here seems no particular reason why, after dumping Marx, we should go on repeating all the nasty things about bourgeois liberalism which he taught us to say."[3] Macherey maintains, by contrast, that a valuable work overcomes the division of public and private life and affects sociohistorical life. Like Foucault, he rightly assumes that what makes a work or a philosophy important is its effective influence on sociohistorical life, not its conformity with objective science or liberal ideals.

While some critics would reduce Macherey's materialism to a postmodern liberalism, others deny it any postmodern import. For example, E. San Juan Jr. claims that it makes possible significant scientific knowledge and ideological critique. Inserting it in "the current world-system conjuncture" would, he says, "test and gauge its . . . precise contribution to enhancing popular movements for radical transformation everywhere" (88). The earlier Althusserian work, which defends a scientific view of history, could, no doubt, contribute to these movements, but the later work, which situates theories within and adopts a partisan view of the oppositions and conflicts defining their context, would not. In fact, in the later *In A Materialist Way* (1998), Macherey praises Foucault because he is "just the opposite of an ideologue of liberation" (101).

Macherey shows, moreover, that, as a practical activity, philosophy is embedded in an institutional context prescribing its forms and limiting its practices. He argues that since the French revolution French philosophy has been inscribed in a republican educational context in which it forms a professional discipline, speaks the national language, and acquires a fixed curriculum and corporate professors. A public, democratic enterprise situated between the educational system's secondary and superior levels, French philosophy initially claimed no positive or disciplinary knowledge but still posed as the judge of other disciplines' claims or the expression of the human spirit. Subsequently, when the success of the sciences threatened to dethrone philosophy, its proponents defended the scientific method against the older, rhetorical or literary form. They also defended modern analytic practices against the Kantian or Hegelian synthetic practices, and scientific knowledge against personal intuition or subjectivity. Macherey claims that he is not criticizing French philosophy, but this history of its origins and its conflicts effectively reveals its institutional limitations, rather than its revolutionary potential.

Of course, philosophy exerts significant influence in Western higher education, which enrolls more than half of the eligible youth, and in the French high school or collège, where, unlike the British or American systems, philosophy is taught in the last year and included on college entrance examinations. A critic might object, however, that, more interested in social mobility and increased consumption than class struggle, theorists who, like Macherey, accept the institutional limits of theory have retreated to academia's cloistered walls and abandoned "popular movements for radical transformation" (see, for example, Reynolds 268 and 274). Such objections preserve the humanist assumption that theory and practice form a unified whole with common values and goals; by contrast, for legitimate historical reasons, including the nightmarish Stalinist practices of the former USSR and of Western communist parties, Althusserians assume that theory is a practice in its own right and possesses its own autonomy. Some Althusserians defend the original notion of a scientific theory or the transformative force of theoretical critique and repudiate any postmodern or Foucauldian influence; others, who, like Macherey as well as Tony Bennett, John Frow, and, to an extent, Althusser himself, critique their earlier belief that science achieves independence of ideology or that theory transforms the practices of social life, show in a Foucauldian manner that the historical development of a discourse explains its diverse schools and movements or its equally diverse accounts of a work's import. As I indicate in the next chapter, Bennett's and Frow's histories of literary study's schools or movements accept recent Anglo-American critiques of the established canon, pedagogical practices, and the traditional curriculum and its gender, racial, and sexual biases and exclusions, whereas, fearing relativism or pluralism, Macherey maintains that "the infinity of contradiction" gives philosophy one

history (*dinosaure* 113). His Foucauldian materialism reveals, nonetheless, the rich history of both literature and
philosophy. More radically than Althusser, he breaks with
his earlier belief that Marxist science has the capacity to
transcend ideology and grasp the essential, historical truth
and, turning partisan, he situates theory within the divided
historical contexts revealing the productive activity and social influence of both writers and readers, both literature
and philosophy.

Post-Marxism and Cultural Studies

The Reception Theory of Tony Bennett and John Frow

Like Pierre Macherey, Tony Bennett, John Frow, and Toby Miller initially adopt Althusserian theory and subsequently develop a Foucauldian view of cultural practices; however, instead of presenting a historical account of misinterpretations or "true errors," Bennett, Frow, and Miller claim that authoritative institutions, what Frow terms "regimes of reading" and Bennett calls "reading formations," constitute modern literary study and govern the reader's interpretive practices. Just as Laclau and Mouffe and Butler promote the democratic articulations of modern social movements, so Bennett, Frow, and Miller support the humanities' women's, black, postcolonial, gay, and cultural programs,; however, Frow and, to an extent, Miller preserve the theoretical self-consciousness defended by Laclau and Mouffe and Butler, whereas, like Macherey or Foucault, Bennett rejects such self-consciousness and depicts the disciplinary practices or "technologies" of modern cultural institutions.

Post-Marxist Reception Theory

Initially, Bennett and Frow elaborate the Althusserian cultural theory of Macherey, who construes literary realism as
the effect of established conventions, not the imitation of an
independent reality. As I noted, Macherey and Balibar grant
that literature reflects reality but argue that the reality reflected by it is the institutional world of discourses and conventions. In *Marxism and Literary History* (1986), Frow
complains that the Althusserian view preserves the transcendent force which traditional Marxism confers upon
sociohistorical reality (28, 38, and 47), but he too argues that
the Althusserians rightly construe realism as an effect of literary discourse, not the author's social conditions (22). In
Outside Literature, Bennett also complains that a scientific
criticism does not reveal a text's "objective" ideological inco-
herence, distortion, and gaps because an ideological subject
cannot adopt the subjectless standpoint of a science especially if, as Althusser says, a science does not constitute a
subject (63–64). Bennett still maintains, however, that great
literature does not conform with an external sociohistorical
context or origin; it produces the effects of realism, as the Althusserians say. He accepts, moreover, Laclau and Mouffe's
claim that the hegemonic force of established discourse undermines the fixed stages and predetermined contexts of traditional Marxist history; as he says, "It becomes difficult to
see how the idea of society can be regarded as supplying a
conceptually 'fixed' or stabilized object" (*Outside* 21).

Liberal historians such as E. D. Hirsch Jr. maintain that
the author's intention represents an autonomous, univer-
sally binding norm, while traditional Marxists claim that an
objective account of the author's social conditions reveals the
historical import of the author's meaning; both the liberals
and the Marxists assume, however, that a text's meaning
transcends established conventions and asserts a profound
truth. Like Macherey, Bennett and Frow deny, by contrast,
that literature achieves such transcendence and, despite
their rejection of Althusserian science, elaborate a scientific
semiotics or Russian formalism.

While many traditional literary historians simply dismissed the formal textual methods, which they attributed to what Lukács derisively labeled "shop talk" and Hirsch called "cognitive atheism," Bennett and Frow take Russian formalism to justify the historical study of literature's institutional conventions. In *Marxism and Formalism* (1979), Bennett argues, for example, that traditional Marxism can learn from Russian formalism, whose accounts of defamiliarization, estrangement, or intertextuality situate texts in a literary context but still subvert established ideological discourses (42–43). In a more scientific fashion, Frow argues that Russian formalism places a text in a "literary series" in which it ruptures with official generic norms and literary codes and affirms its own vision. A modernist practice fostered by commodity production, the estrangement or, in structuralist terms, "intertextuality" of the Russian formalists subverts the conventional opposition between intrinsic literary practices and extrinsic scientific, legal, political, religious, or economic discourse.

In *The Prison-House of Language*, Fredric Jameson acknowledges that semiotics and Russian formalism reveal the cultural models or ideological sign systems mediating between literature and society, as Bennett and Frow say, but he complains that in a positivist fashion semiotics and Russian formalism construct an autonomous, synchronic, or systematic view of language divorced from the contingent diachronic or historical view. I grant that Bennett and Frow adopt such a positivist or scientific formalism and dismiss history in Jameson's broad Hegelian sense; however, despite the Russian formalism, Bennett and Frow consider literature a historical construct with changing genres and sociohistorical import.

For instance, Bennett denies that literature possesses a timeless essence that includes only a few established genres and reveals the universal truths of our human nature, as traditional critics say; rather, citing Raymond Williams, he shows that literature's canonical genres and texts and opposition to nonliterary discourses have changed markedly especially in the twentieth century, when the media have so heavily influenced the reader's practices (*Formalism* 15). Similarly, Frow says that literature is not an autonomous entity composed of a few unchanging genres; literary texts have an ideological or sociohistorical import and changing genres and types (101–102).

Jameson also discusses literature's changing genres and forms, yet, since he preserves the romantic notion of authorial genius, he argues that a properly historicized linguistics describes and evaluates cultural models or paradigms, which, embedded in the author's unconscious, "mediate" between text and society.[1] Although Bennett and Frow reject Jameson's broad, Hegelian notion of history, they too consider Russian formalism and literary history compatible; however, they take Russian formalism to legitimate the interpretive activity of readers, not this romantic faith in the author's profundity. For example, Frow claims that intertextuality opens a place for reading, which constitutes the text's references to codes, genres, other texts, and nonliterary discourses. Hans Robert Jauss also takes Russian formalism to show that interpretations reveal the reader's repertoire of commitments, beliefs, and aesthetic ideals, but he claims that, by virtue of a hermeneutics of self and other, readers can still grasp the radically incommensurate meanings of the historical author provided that the text distances the reader from or defamiliarizes the conventions of his epoch. Like Macherey, who argues that, "true errors," a reader's mistaken interpretations realize the text's import, Frow claims, by contrast, that criticism does not refute wrong interpretations or reveal the historical author's original meaning; rather, they illuminate the intertextual literary system or "regime of reading" governing a reader's interpretations.

Frow fears, however, that, because the "regimes of reading" that govern the reception of diverse literatures or cultures are incommensurable, these regimes generate a vitiating relativism that renders all judgments of value equivalent, ignores differences within communities, and permits no "*critique* of everyday processes" (*Studies* 132). As a consequence, like Laclau and Mouffe and Butler, Frow defends the aesthetic self-consciousness enabling "cultural intellectuals" to grasp their determining sociohistorical interests as a class (*Studies* 165-69), and readers to resist the established codes, genres, and norms of their regimes of reading; as he says, "The productive role of the reader . . . represents a break with a dominant regime of reading and with the institutional context which directly or indirectly sustains this regime" (*Marxism* 229).

Bennett too maintains that the intertextuality of Russian formalism or contemporary semiotics opens a place for reading, but he denies that the productive reader breaks "with a dominant regime of reading" and its sustaining "institutional context"; rather, like Jauss, who grants in his later work that art that conforms with its conventions also produces pleasure, he claims that authoritative institutions regulate the reader's activity. In keeping with Foucault's claim that the genealogy of a discourse reveals its internal divisions and ruptures, he says that "[t]o think critically about criticism requires that account be taken of the actual mechanisms of the literary-pedagogical apparatus . . . inducting the reader into the socially constructed interior of the text as a space in which to exhibit not correct readings but a *way* of reading" (*Outside* 189). A text provides "a space in which to exhibit not correct readings but a *way* of reading" because literary study's authoritative mechanisms or "reading formations" govern the reader's interpretive activity.[2] To interpret a text is to contest a text's terrain, to vindicate one's methods and ideologies, and, by implication if not by explicit assertion, to debunk opposed methods and ideologies.

Moreover, like Macherey, who says that theory is always situated and never pure, independent, or scientific, Bennett repudiates not only the formal autonomy justified by a scientific semiotics but also the theoretical self-consciousness defended by Frow as well as Laclau and Mouffe and Butler. For example, Bennett claims that the traditional aesthetics of David Hume, Immanuel Kant, and other modern theorists requires but fails to establish absolute norms of universal value. Indeed, he and Barbara Herrnstein Smith critique "foundational" aesthetics in a similar manner. Smith emphasizes the individuality of the reader, whose personal "economy" of values justify his or her judgments and interpretations, and faults modern literary study, whose oppressive aesthetic "axiology" precludes such individual judgments of value, while Bennett says that established reading formations enable schools and universities to discipline readers, ensuring that they constitute proper subjects; still, Bennett and Smith both claim that the traditional aesthetics of Hume, Kant, and other modern theorists requires but fails to establish absolute norms of universal value (*Outside* 143–67 and *Contingencies* 54–85). For instance, Smith and Bennett expose the inconsistency of David Hume, who claims that different persons, cultures, and eras show a remarkable diversity of taste, but who insists that humankind also shows an equally remarkable uniformity of judgment. Hume argues that the sensitivity, training, and impartiality of an authoritative critic ensure the universal validity of his or her judgments, yet he admits that even these critics may not agree. Smith and Bennett find a comparable inconsistency in Kant, who claims that individual judgments of value must employ the universal terms "good" and "bad" even though these judgments are subjective and hypothetical. Critics talk as though everyone must share their taste, yet only the hypothetical assumption of a common human nature or a common sense gives these subjective judgments their universality. Both Smith and Bennett also fault the Critical Theory of the Frankfurt School, whose accounts of ideological distortions or false consciousness preserve bourgeois notions of universal truth, as well as traditional Marxists, who expect judgments of value to possess universal validity but whose historical "grand narrative" also fails to overcome the opposition between universal values and a critic's subjective taste.

Peggy Kamuf complains that this critique of aesthetic judgment treats it as real, not hypothetical: in her terms, Bennett tends "to read Kant as invoking a substantive understanding, *our own*" (33; see also Guillory 273). This objection mixes up theoretical ideals and institutional practices. It is not Bennett or Smith but the received reading formations that affirm the universal truths of common sense or

our human nature or treat them as our "substantive understanding." Kamuf assumes, moreover, that in a Kantian
manner Bennett means to free literature from its institutional technology (31). It is true that in the relatively early
"Texts in History" (1985), Bennett takes Marxist reception
study to disrupt the institutional reproduction of established
ideologies and to situate texts in "different reading formations," which in Laclau and Mouffe's fashion he identifies
with contemporary working-class, feminist, and African
American movements; nonetheless, in later work, he considers the institutional technology of literary study positive or
enabling, not oppressive or "functionalist."

More fully than Frow, Bennett limits the constitutive
force of theoretical ideals and acknowledges the governmental policies or technologies of power regulating cultural institutions.[3] He complains, for example, that, while Laclau
and Mouffe show that discourse undermines the Marxist science of society, they reduce "politics to a struggle for the
rhetorical construction of the social" (*Outside* 264). They fail,
as a result, to recognize that "particular regions of social life
are characterized by a definite positivity whereby conduct is
regulated, norms legislated, competing claims adjudicated,
decisions made, programs planned and implemented and so
forth" (*Outside* 267).

He shows, for example, that during the nineteenth
century, when the schools turned literature into a "moral
technology," the ideal teacher and, subsequently, the inde-
cipherable text made the reader's interpretive activity the
basis of his or her unending ethical improvement (*Outside*
177–80). Authoritative literary institutions impose on the
reader the textual norms requiring an endless pursuit of
self-improvement. As he says,

> To think critically about criticism requires that ac-
> count be taken of the actual mechanisms of the lit-
> erary-pedagogical apparatus . . . inducting the
> reader into the socially constructed interior of the
> text as a space in which to exhibit not correct read-
> ings but a *way* of reading in relation to norms

which, since their essence consists in their capacity
for endless revision, can never be precisely speci-
fied. (*Outside* 189)

The aesthetic norms of the text do not transcend literary institutions, as traditional critics say; rather, a text provides "a
space in which to exhibit not correct readings but a *way* of
reading" because literary study's authoritative mechanisms
or "reading formations" impose on the reader indeterminate
norms capable of "endless revision." Marxist, poststructuralist, and some reader-oriented critics also expect this endless
interpretive activity to ensure the reader's improvement, but
these critics too ignore the power of this literary technology
to constitute a self-improving subject.

Moreover, he demonstrates that, in defense of theoretical critique or self-consciousness, radical theorists reduce
cultural institutions to a political instrument or to a threat-
ening co-optation and ignore the positive governmental policies implemented by them. In *Culture: A Reformer's Science*
(1998), for example, he critiques the Gramscian notion that,
creating political assent or imposing "hegemony," culture
emanates from a centering social formation and integrates
and mediates diverse levels of social organization (76–77);
rather, various technologies produce various cultural resources and impose equally various forms and kinds of discipline or governmental organization (69–70; see also Toby
Miller, *Self*). Libraries, television, movies, or museums do
not form a unified subject functioning as a coherent agent of
social change; they form subjects with diverse economic,
political, or literary kinds of loyalty or normality.

Bennett takes these diverse technologies to impose governmental policies that he considers liberal in the sense that
their results come from subjects changing themselves,
rather than from the ruling class' hegemonic discourse. He
shows, for example, that in the nineteenth century British
and American reformers expected public libraries and art
museums to reform the working man, whose visits to them
would move him to stop frequenting ale houses and to im-
prove himself and through him his wife and his family (*Sci-*

ence 124–28). In the early twentieth century, staffed by geologists, historians, anthropologists, and archaeologists and integrated into the public school curriculum, the new natural history museums acquired more importance than art museums or libraries because the Darwinian history museums encouraged the social mobility or restlessness of working people (*Science* 155–64).

Indeed, Bennett and Toby Miller both maintain that established discourses constitute normal or "civil" subjects or, in literary contexts, reading practices and formations, rather than oppositional or subversive agents. In a Foucauldian manner, Bennett and Miller suggest that, rooted in institutional practices, literary discourse evolves distinct historical configurations of power and knowledge or, in conventional language, of diverse schools or interpretive communities.

Miller argues that various technologies produce cultural resources imposing equally various forms of normality. Libraries, television, movies, or academic disciplines, especially economics, political science, and literary criticism, constitute subjects loyal to what he terms the "cultural-capitalist state"; however, since the state is not absolutist, these disciplines and cultural practices form subjects with diverse economic, political, or literary kinds of loyalty or normality, not a unified subject functioning as a coherent agent of social change.

Miller's account of the "cultural-capitalist state" forcefully characterizes the institutional technologies not only of the academic disciplines but also of television, movies, and other popular cultural forms. Moreover, Miller shows that the ethical norms and textual incompleteness or indeterminacy of cultural study ensure that, to complete themselves, readers accept the ideals of the state. His belief that a totalizing episteme underlines diverse disciplines or discourses and explains their "rules of formation" (see *Self* xvii) neglects, just the same, Foucault's distinction between an archaeology, which explains the broad episteme underlying and justifying the norms and procedures of established discourses, and a genealogy, which reveals the local institutional contexts in which a discourse has evolved and acquired legitimacy. In other words, a genealogy describes a discourse's ruptures, divisions, and conflicts, whereas Miller treats cultural study as a unified technology imposing the same ethical norms and textual indeterminacy. Moreover, instead of defending the new programs of the multicultural university, he adopts the traditional notion that, since the late eighteenth century, when literary studies was a crucial site of the human sciences, it has suffered a decline (*Self* 68–69).

Not only does Bennett, by contrast, defend the political vitality of educational and cultural institutions, he critiques the revolutionary pretensions of radical theorists. For example, he maintains that "[w]ork in educational institutions, which involve extended populations for increasingly lengthy periods of their life cycles, is in no way to be downgraded or regarded as less vital politically than the attempt to produce new collective forms of cultural association" (*Outside* 239). While Stuart Hall argues that cultural studies must resist its disciplinary contexts if it is to avoid cooptation, Bennett esteems its established institutional status, which includes not only academic programs with specific course requirements but also a growing industry of classroom textbooks and scholarly journals and studies (*Culture* 20). Fredric Jameson expects cultural studies to form a historic bloc of progressive academic and public radicals, whereas Bennett argues that in most colleges and universities, which are under strict state regulation, cultural studies can, at best, contribute to a student's general education requirements and employment prospects (*Culture* 32).

The vast expansion of the modern university and the increased accessibility of the humanities, not to mention unfriendly legislatures and heightened public opposition and political scrutiny, clearly justify this defense of educational institutions; nonetheless, even though the growth of women's, black, gay, and cultural studies has sharply divided the humanities, Bennett says that the "institutional placement" of modern intellectuals in "tertiary educational institutions" allows only formal practices, rather than a progressive politics (*Culture* 32). This notion of "institutional placement" involves what Miller terms "redemption through a neo-Wittgenstein-ian concept of rule rather than neoromantic elevations of resistance" (*Technologies* 72). That is, the notion of placement implies that criticism remains neutral and independent even though contrary reading formations so sharply divide the humanities, especially in the United States. Here it is not political self-consciousness but the multicultural orientation of the modern university that justifies the new women's, black, cultural, gay, or ethnic programs and studies. Contrary to Bennett, who takes educational policies to nullify any political practices, and to Laclau and Mouffe and Butler, who expect theoretical critique to promote the democratic articulation or translation of "empty" universals, the educational policies establishing and maintaining these studies support these contemporary social movements but do not impose self-conscious theoretical norms.

Consider, for example, the controversial reception of Sara Paretsky's feminist detective fiction. As reviewers point out, her novels have been very popular, with many weeks on the best-seller lists, publication in thirteen countries, and a world-wide network of fan clubs. What explains this popularity is the fiction's changing institutional context or "reading formations." That is, while conventional detective novels conform with their generic formulas and chauvinist ideology and satisfy in this way their high school educated, male, working-class readers, Paretsky's novels challenge these chauvinist formulas and, as a result, appeal to modern women readers, who have a college education and professional status.

Erin Smith says that, because the hardboiled detective's secretary shows an ambiguous gender—like Hammer's Velda, sexy but often violent too—the feminist detective fiction of the 1980s and 1990s is implicit in the 1930s fiction (168), whose male, working-class readers faced, Smith indicates, the historic loss of the artisan's economic autonomy, the growth of fast-paced industrial production, the increased economic independence of women, and the pursuit of middle-class comfort and social mobility. It is true that Paretsky's fiction elaborates the wiseguy manner, confrontational investigation, angry ranting, and other conventions of hardboiled detective fiction, but Smith's argument fails to acknowledge how drastically conditions have changed since the 1930s or to explain why women's hardboiled fiction should grow so explosively popular in the 1970s and 1980s. The reason is that, as Priscilla Walton and Manina Jones suggest, moving well beyond secretarial positions, college-educated, professional Anglo-American women, who since the 1990s attend college in greater numbers than men do, appreciate depictions of strong women (22–30, 121–27). What explains the popularity is not only the modern education of professional women, but also the new academic status of popular culture. That is, no longer restricted to popular or "pulp" magazines, detective fiction is studied in modern English departments, where courses in cultural studies and women's literature expose the ideological import of detective fiction's conventions.

The changing nature of the fiction's readership, the subversion of established conventions, and the academic studies of popular culture explain and justify the popularity of Paretsky's fiction and, by implication, modern, multicultural movements. Bennett denies this political import even though he appreciates the institutional value of such studies. While Frow and Miller support such studies and their politics, Frow and Miller, like Laclau and Mouffe and Butler, preserve theoretical self-consciousness. By contrast, like Macherey's materialism, Bennett's Foucauldian histories limit or reject theory's transformative force and, despite the dismissal of cultural politics, profoundly depict the changing contexts of Anglo-American "reading formations."

Conclusion

As I have indicated, influenced by Althusser and Foucault, the work of Tony Bennett, Judith Butler, John Frow, Ernesto LaClau, Pierre Macherey, Chantal Mouffe, Stephen Resnick, Robert Wolff, and others critiques traditional Marxist notions of class context and economic determination and assimilates poststructuralist concepts of discourse or power/knowledge. Among the most successful Marxist work in decades, *Empire*, by Michael Hardt and Antonio Negri, also adopts the poststructuralist theory of Michel Foucault, who claims that local complexes of knowledge and power, not the economic base, discipline society, and of Jacques Derrida, who argues that that Marx's "hauntology" undermines the traditional Marxist opposition between materialist science and idealist speculations. Of course, from Lenin to Marcuse, many, many works have radically challenged the Marxist tradition, including its claim that historical development will reduce capitalist society to two main classes: the few, rich bourgeoisie and the many, poor working people, and that revolution will take place in the advanced industrial countries and will be led by the industrial working class. What distinguishes *Empire*'s revisions of the tradition is that it also repudiates Lenin's belief that imperialism is the highest stage of capitalism as well as Marx's belief that the global market preserves the Western bourgeoisie's national sovereignty and that the organized working class would lead the struggle for socialism. Moreover, *Empire* describes a new global order in which transnational forces, including labor, production, and bio-political

109

power, dominate the world and provoke the spontaneous resistance of multitudes.

Abdul-Karim Mustapha and Bülent Eken say that "*Empire* is definitely a Marxist project but one that radically questions the aspirations of that tradition and its meanings today" (3); however, preserving the traditional priority of economic processes, *Empire* goes on to show that global capital's fluid character or productive strategies assimilate poststructuralist theory and justify the resistance of unorganized masses. Michael Ryan rightly objects to this critique: "Now I for one have trouble believing that Rupert Murdoch checks his old copy of *Grammatology* for tips on how to rule"(6). In addition, unlike the post-Marxists, who, for the most part, reveal the sexual, racial, class, and ethnic divisions of Western society and support the oppositional movements of women, blacks, gays, and others, Hardt and Negro claim that "[t]he contemporary gurus of corporate culture . . . [p]reach the efficiency and profitability of diversity and multiculturalism within corporations" (cited in Ryan 6). In other words, in the traditional manner that I discussed in the introduction, they subordinate black, women's, or ethnic movements to the class struggle. As Ryan says, their critique of poststructuralist theory "spills over into an attack on multiculturalism, which is also seen as a tool of capitalism" (6).

Althusser argued that the many schools and movements in philosophy are open to political critique, what he calls class struggle in theory, but did not abandon the traditional view of economic determination in that last instance or stop supporting the working class and its political parties. More fully than Hardt and Negri, post-Marxists repudiate this view of economic determination and working-class politics. The post-Marxists elaborate the partisan, overdetermined, figural, or subjective import of historical, sexual, aesthetic, cultural, and philosophical discourse; however, some of these post-Marxists preserve the ideals of theoretical subversion and, faulting the conformist "functionalism" of institutional approaches, advocate a new hegemonic bloc of independent black, women's, ethnic, gay, or trade union movements, while others repudiate the norms of theory and emphasize the institutional rituals or disciplines of the established institutions constructing the subject.

The most emphatic opposition to theoretical critique stems from Michel Foucault, who maintains that the changing institutional contexts and the ruptures or gaps in a discourse's historical development, not the autonomous norms nor the objective truths of a scientific theory, explain the history of a discourse and open it to critique. The most emphatic defense of theoretical critique comes from Ernesto Laclau and Chantal Mouffe, who claim that the ideological apparatuses of the state interpellate or construct a subject and, thereby, reproduce themselves, as Althusser maintains, but who defend a poststructuralist version of ideological hegemony, not the Foucauldian notion of power/knowledge, because they fear that it imposes a functionalist conformity. In Laclau's semiotic terms, the subject remains fissured because the antagonisms of the women's, black, gay, ethnic, or trade union movements or the dislocation of social structures matters more than the systematic contradictions and predetermined structures of traditional Marxism (*Hegemony* 122–34).

Just as the Foucauldian notion of power/knowledge opposes theoretical critique, so the theoretical critique of Laclau and Mouffe opposes the Foucauldian notion of power/knowledge; nonetheless, Judith Butler adopts both. She claims that Althusser's notion of interpellation and Foucault's theory of subjugation justify her belief that the heterosexual norms imposed by power govern the construction of gender. She takes Althusser's and Foucault's views to suggest that gender is a matter of a performance imposed by established cultural norms. She grants that the heterosexual norms imposed by institutional power preclude the political liberation sought by oppositional theorists, yet she still adopts Freudian or Lacanian notions of the unconscious as well as post-Marxist versions of a radical democracy. While the Freudian notions contradict or, as she says, "supplement" the Foucauldian approach, making subjugation the desire of the complicitous subject, not a social construct, the post-Marxist account democratizes her notion of gender, opening it to articulation by African American, third world, and other peoples of color.

Pierre Macherey also adopts Althusserian Marxism and Foucauldian poststructuralism; however, since he repudiates the Freudian, Nietzschean, and Hegelian modes of theoretical critique defended by Butler and Laclau and Mouffe, his post-Marxist materialism achieves greater historical depth. Like other post-Marxists, Macherey initially defends the Althusserian belief that scientific Marxism opposes Stalinist and humanist theory, but he shows that literature, situated between science and ideology, reveals but does not tell the truth. In his later work, he adopts what he calls a materialist perspective, which, inspired by Michel Foucault, maintains that, never pure, independent, or scientific, theory is always situated in a practical context in which it reveals the antagonisms of and takes a position on the contrary views forming the context. While Laclau and Mouffe and Butler promote the radically democratizing articulations or translations of the women's, black, postcolonial or other new social movements, Macherey defends a philosophical realism that denies the incommensurable, "relativist" perspectives of such movements; nonetheless, achieving great historical depth, Macherey argues in the later work that the productive activities not only of authors but of readers give a literary or a philosophical text its meaning and, despite or because of their errors, their accounts explain its history.

The cultural theory of Tony Bennett, John Frow, and Toby Miller also rejects the scientific theory of the Althusserian tradition and in Bennett's and Miller's case develops a Foucauldian account of cultural practices. Like Pierre Macherey, Bennett and Frow initially elaborate Althusserian cultural theory, which construes literary realism as the effect of established conventions, not the imitation of an independent reality. Bennett and Frow also go on to show that the interpretive practices of readers explain a text's import and, more generally, literature's history; however, like Laclau and Mouffe and Butler, Frow defends the subversive force of critical theory, while, more radically than Macherey, Bennett and Miller emphasize the historical and institutional contexts of cultural policy or practices. Moreover, even though Bennett overlooks the political divisions of the modern Anglo-American university, he rightly esteems the cultural programs established in it.

In general, the work of Judith Butler, Pierre Macherey, Ernesto LaClau, Chantal Mouffe, Tony Bennett, John Frow and Toby Miller suggests that, unlike traditional Marxism, which emphasizes the priority of class struggle and the common humanity of oppressed groups, the post-Marxism deriving from Althusser and Foucault reveals the sexual, racial, class, and ethnic divisions of modern Western society. Those post-Marxists who preserve the normative ideals of Freudian, Hegelian, Derridean, or critical theory and dismiss the institutional contexts of their discursive practices forcefully justify the radically democratic articulations, translations, or potential hegemony of oppositional or independent movements. Those post-Marxists who repudiate the ideals of theoretical critique and emphasize the socio-historical contexts of modern discursive practices open these practices to political critique. More precisely, this antitheoretical approach supports the progressive organizations that have been successfully established, and, as a result, this approach too effectively promotes the progressive transformation of Western social life.

Notes

Introduction: From Marx to Post-Marxism

1. In a similar vein, Michael Awkward says, "Wright's view of literature [e.g., as a "blunt weapon"], along with his apparent lack of interest in the significance of female oppression, rendered him unable to appreciate Hurston's subtle critiques of ... American society" (12). Henry Louis Gates Jr., says that "[w]hat we might think of as Hurston's mythic realism, lush and dense within a lyrical black idiom, seemed politically retrograde to the proponents of a social or critical realism" ("Afterward" 190). Gates adds that Hurston's "complexity . . . refuses to lend itself to the glib categories of 'radical' or 'conservative,' 'black' or 'negro,' 'revolutionary' or 'Uncle Tom'—categories of little use in literary criticism" ("Afterward" 186).

2. 70; see also Stuart Sim, who says, "[T]he decline in importance, both socially and politically, of the working class . . . has obvious implications for the growth of a post-Marxist consciousness, given the critical role that classical Marxism allotted the work class as the 'gravediggers of capitalism'" (5). Sim is right, but an equally important social development is the independent black, feminist, gay, ethnic, or postcolonial movements because their emergence shows that the interests and policies of oppositional groups involve much more than class context or struggle.

3. See Paul Walton and Andrew Gamble, who say that Marx's account of capitalism's "laws of motion . . . are firmly derived from his labor theory of value" (200), and Ronald Meek, who says that Adam Smith "formulated a new concept of surplus in which profit was . . . ascribed to the productivity of labour in general; and he outlined a new theory of the development of society

and the nature of socio-historical processes in general which . . . set the stage for the eventual emergence of the materialist conception of history" (16).

4. Terry Carver says, for example, that a skeptic is in "a strong position to unravel the narrative on which so much Marxist orthodoxy depends, by working backwards from the differences that textual comparisons between Marx and Engels can plausibly establish" (see *The Postmodern Marx* 173). Carver also says that the biographical frame imposed on Marx's texts "presents a 'master image' dating from late in life, when the master's 'thought' is presumed to have matured from germs of intimation traceable in early writings. This practice . . . validates visually a teleological reading of an author's work, valuing early materials just as 'steps on the way' to something only fully realized at some presumed culmination . . . in Marx's case, the presumed culmination has, since Engels, been conceptualized as a doctrinal system issuing forth from a scientist/philosopher" (164). Similarly, Munck says that the "religion of Marxism-Leninism" comes from Engels, not Marx, whose method, "that of radical critique, with its inherent capacity of reflexivity and self-critique," anticipates "all the radical trends in epistemology, from feminism to deconstruction" (5).

5. See Dennis Dworkin, 10–44. For a contrary view, see Ivo Kamps, who maintains that "poststructuralist theory" made it possible for the "so-called 'vulgar' Marxism to rethink the relationship between principles of determination, human agency, and the creation and reception of works of art" (1).

6. See Auerbach, 333, and Roger Chartier, 71–108. Other scholars have suggested that, instituted in the public schools, where Matthew Arnold was chief inspector for twenty years, this humanism stifled the rebellion and the opposition of women and the working class, imposed bourgeois forms of national unity and, by the 1880s and 1890s, adopted racist and anti-Semitic tones (see Chris Baldick 82; Doyle 12; Martin Bernal I: 347–66; and Gerald Graff, *Professing* 12–13).

7. See also John Brenkman, who argues that the liberal, critical and positivist, Stalinist stances are not compatible. The evils of Soviet communism teach us that in *The German Ideology* Marx naively united these two incompatible stances (61).

8. See, for example, Marie Fleming, who says that Habermas's "theory of communicative action does not allow for the articulation" of a "vision of gender equality" (1).

Chapter 1. Economics and Theory

1. Studies of his life and works include Ted Benton's *The Rise and Fall of Structuralist Marxism* (1984), Gregory Elliot's *Althusser: The Detour of Theory* (1987), Robert Paul Resch's *Althusser and the Renewal of Marxist Social Theory* (1992), and Stephen B. Smith's *Reading Althusser* (1984). Literary anthologies that reproduce his essays include Hazard Adams's *Critical Theory since 1965* (1986), Anthony Easthope and Kate McGowan's *A Critical and Cultural Theory Reader* (1992), and Dan Lattimer's *Contemporary Critical Theory* (1989); and surveys that examine Althusser's work include Michèle Barrett's *The Politics of Truth* (1991), Art Berman's *From the New Criticism to Deconstruction* (1988), Anthony Easthope's *British Post-structuralism* (1988), John Frow's *Marxism and Literary History* (1986), my *The Politics of Literary Theory* (1990), Richard Harland's *Superstructuralism*, Diane MacDowell's *Theories of Discourse* (1986), and Michael Sprinker's *Imaginary Relations* (1987). Distinguished literary theorists who adopted Althusserian views include Fredric Jameson, Terry Eagleton, Catherine Belsey, and Tony Bennett. Jorge Larrain says that "Althusser's influence . . . practically covers the whole gamut of the social sciences. An impressive number of academics and intellectuals working in anthropology, philosophy, sociology, political science, linguistics, semiology, semantics, cultural studies, literary criticism, criminology and psychology have been affected by Althusser in one way or another" (67).

2. As Steven Best and Douglas Kellner say, in this work Lyotard "carries through a linguistic and philosophical turn which renders his theory more and more abstract and distanced from the social realities and problems of the present age" (165).

3. "Structural" 112. In "Modernism, Postmodernism, and Social Theory," Robert Resch also grants that in *Reading Capital*, where Althusser distinguishes between philosophy and science, he rejects the foundational status of theory (531). Indeed, Resch shows that Althusser considers the Hegelian or Sartrian notions of praxis and of mediations the mythic ideal of a general, unified practice. Resch complains, nonetheless, that postmodern "irrationalists" reject "economic determination and class struggle as explanatory principles" and show a "hostility to Marxism . . . whose significance can hardly be understated" (*Althusser* 5). See also Anderson 33; Benton 177–82; Callinicos, "Living" 41; Elliot, *Detour*; Montag, "What is at Stake" 102.

4. Like Resnick and Wolff, Anthony Callari and David Ruccio grant that Althusser's critique of classical Marxism initiates a post-modern Marxism whose repudiation of "grand narratives" and critique of systematic Marxism parallel the work of Lyotard and others (32–40). Callari and Ruccio forcefully demonstrate that this post-Marxism allows the heterogeneity, alternative cultures, and diverse racial, sexual, and ethnic identities denied by homogenizing classical Marxism, whose insistence that capitalism and communism occupy a uniform economic space explains the failures of the Soviet experiment (13). To keep Marxism viable, Callari and Ruccio argue, however, that postmodernism does not rupture neatly with modernism but, to remain radical or, at least, not bourgeois, depends upon traditional or "modernist" Marxism (26–28). While Althusser argues that, because foundational ideals have broken down, diverse discourses or schools reveal incommensurable ideals, methods, or frameworks, Callari and Ruccio reconstitute Marx's traditional notions of value, socialism, the working class, the vanguard, and so on. Callari and Ruccio attribute these notions to traditional and post-Marxism and, thereby, deny their incompatibility; however, what is important about Althusser's post-Marxism is just this recognition that without the traditional foundational ideals the contemporary era can no longer reconcile the discourses or rhetorics of diverse discourses or movements.

Chapter 2. From Archaeology to Genealogy

1. For example, in *Soundings in Critical Theory*, Dominick LaCapra voices many familiar criticisms of Althusser: his subtle "positivist" scientism locates ideology in the subject, makes ideology necessary or inevitable, treats the theorist's transcendance as unproblematic, and ignores or denies the ideological character of objective, subjectless science (13, 166). By contrast, he grants that Foucault's concept of power/knowledge forcefully reveals "the complicity of forces that are often neatly separated, especially in defense of a value-neutral, unworldly contemplative idea of research," yet he insists that the genuine critic opposes the "black functionalism" whereby "'the system' or the 'dominant ideology'... necessarily 'co-opts' everything it touches, including all forms of resistance."

Similarly, Poster grants that Althusser and Foucault promote the specialized knowledge of the modern scientific, academic, or "specific" intellectual. In *Foucault, Marxism, and History*, Poster admits that Althusser's critique of the subject and of ideology parallels Foucault's accounts of the subject and of discourse/practice, but Poster still rejects Althusser's account of ideology because Poster assumes that Marxists address only the past era of factory production, not the modern era of electronic communication. That is to say, since electronics has made the modern era what Poster calls an era of communication, he dismisses the work of Althusser or any other Marxists—their unchanging theories of economic production cannot explain or resist totalitarian or other modern forms of domination. By contrast, Poster esteems the work of Foucault, who, Poster says, preserves resistance either as local opposition within evolving discourses or as rupture between a discourse's ancient and modern versions. All the same, Poster laments Foucault's lack of historical and methodological self-consciousness even though such self-consciousness dismisses the specialized contexts of Foucault's work and reaffirms the systematic, totalizing thought of the traditional Hegelian intellectual. For a similar critique, see Steven Best and Douglas Kellner 68–72; Fredric Jameson, "Regarding Postmodernism" 39, and "On 'Cultural Studies'" 45–46; Michael Sprinker, "The War" 109–11; Henry Giroux 137; Edward; Said 243–44; Nicos Poulantzas 36, 44; and Michael Walzer 54–55, 61.

Similarly, Michèle Barrett praises Foucault's account of discourse, power, the body, and subjectivity but condemns Althusser's account of ideology and theory. She admits that Althusser rejects classical Marxism's reductive division of base and superstructure, its fabled unity of theory and practice, and even its reductive forms of economic determination. She recognizes that in a Foucauldian manner Althusser endows ideology with a constitutive import which the classical division of base/superstructure denies; however, she still assumes that Marxism does not respond to the serious epistemological difficulties posed by Soviet communism. In fact, more negative than traditional Marxists and critical theorists, she argues that, unlike Foucault, whose accounts of subjectivity or the body overcome these difficulties, an unchanging and unchangeable Marxism endlessly repeats the same errors and poses the same dangers. Lastly, she too considers Althusser's account of ideological reproduction "functionalist," but she claims that his account precludes the subversive activities of teachers, scholars, or artists because she finds the idea of an academic politics inherently ridiculous—he presents "immensely pretentious" arguments about "sitting thinking" (Barrett 36; see also Kitching 82–95).

2. Alan Sheridan details the polemical thunderbolts that Foucault and Marxists have hurled at each other. In "Foucault's Dilemma," John Rajchman finds leftist inclinations but little leftist substance in Foucault's work. Charles Lemert and Garth Gillian discover some but not very much Marxist thought in Foucault. Richard Marsden says that "Marxists loathe the postmodern, relativist, discourse-analyzing Foucault. Foucauldians scorn the modern, economistic, state-centered Marx" (25). Marsden shows that Marx's account of capital and Foucault's account of disciplinary power complement each other (177–92) but repudiates the Foucauldian or postmodern belief "that an objective reality has gone and that the rules of argument have changed" (25).

3. As Gilles Deleuze says, Foucault reads Heidegger through Nietzsche: the will to power explains the ability of language to bring what is into the open or the clearing where it becomes visible even as it recedes into darkness (120).

4. As Walzer says, "Some kind of functionalist Marxism . . . provides the distant underpinning of Foucault's account of power" (57). MacDowell and Smart claim that Gramsci's notion of hegemony plays this role of underpinning (MacDowell 103–104; Smart, "Politics" 159–60).

5. For a thorough account of these objections, see Gary Gutting's "Foucault and the History of Madness."

6. See Marsden, who says that "Foucault's criticism of power in terms of law and the state" complements Marx's "criticism of the juridic self-understanding of the monads of civil society" (192).

7. Drawing on Marx's *Capital*, Marsden explains and elaborates these parallels of capital and disciplinary techniques (149–76).

8. See also Anthony Easthope, who grants that in similar ways Althusser and Foucault undermine humanist theory and explain the arbitrary ideological or historical constitution of the subject (83–84, 134); nonetheless, to overcome the "functionalism" of their accounts and give oppositional theory the power to resist modern society's technocratic discourse and reified institutions, Easthope rejects Foucault's determination to fold subjectivity into a "vaguely defined notion of power" and, like Laclau and Mouffe and Butler, favors the Lacanian theory that ideological recognition is invariably misrecognition or fantasy expressing repressed desire (218).

9. See *Foucault and Feminism*, in which Lois McNay argues that, formulating a relational notion of identity, Foucault's work on sexuality opens the possibility of a radical democracy in which various subjectivities form a democratic coalition (111). Such claims

grant Foucault's later work the emancipatory import that Ernesto Laclau and Chantal Mouffe attribute to a radical, democracy based on the Enlightenment tradition. See also Sawicki.

Chapter 3. Post-Marxism and Democracy

1. As Slavoj Žižek says, "The real achievement of *Hegemony* is crystalized in the concept of 'social antagonism'" ("Beyond Discourse-Analysis" 249).

2. Traditional Marxists grant that the Stalinist regime acquired a dogmatic, oppressive character but deny that their broad dialectical view of history has anything to do with one-sided Stalinist dogma—certainly Georg Lukács, who supported the Stalinist regime and still praised Solzhenitsyn's dissident fiction, mistakenly believed the Soviet government would evolve, not collapse. Frankfurt School theorists also admit that Stalinist communism was dogmatic and oppressive, but they claim that the whole modern world is equally oppressive because they consider Enlightenment reason totalitarian. Scientific Althusserians also consider Stalinist communism oppressive and dogmatic but simply dismiss totalitarian theory—Robert Resch calls it an "oxymoronic anti-Marxist myth" catering to middle-class fears (17).

3. Some liberal totalitarian theorists grant that the Soviet Union applied Marx's account of history's laws and socialism's inevitability but maintain that Soviet communism violates Marx's humanist ideals. In *Today's Isms: Communism, Fascism, Capitalism, Socialism*, which reached its ninth edition in 1985, William Ebenstein and Edwin Fogelman say, for example, that Soviet communism elaborates but deforms Western ideals. Although they admit that Marx had humanist leanings and that Lenin developed a Russian viewpoint, they still explain Soviet communism as the systematic application of Marx's "principles." See also James R. Ozinga's *Communism: The Story of the Idea and Its Implementation*, 2nd Ed., Englewood Cliffs, NJ: Prentice-Hall, 1991 72–94.

4. See also the influential *The End of Ideology Debate* (1968), where Daniel Bell describes communist doctrine as "total ideology," which is "an all-inclusive system of comprehensive reality" and which, as a "secular religion", permits "the assertion of the self . . . in the domination over others" (96–97).

5. As Laclau says, "Lacan is not only, for me, a poststructuralist, but also one of the two crucial moments in the emergence

of a poststructuralist theoretical terrain. The other is deconstruction, of course" (*Contingency* 74).

Chapter 4. Sex, Gender, and Philosophy

1. 3; see also Toril Moi, who says that "one may arrive at a highly historicized and concrete understanding of bodies and subjectivity without relying on the sex/ gender distinction that Butler takes as axiomatic, and particularly without entering into the obscure and theoreticist debates about materiality and meaning that her understanding of sex and gender compels her to engage with" (46).

2. In *Bodies that matter*, she says, for example, that the process of subjectivation outlined by Foucault is in need of psychoanalytic rethinking (189). In *The Psychic Life of Power*, she argues that, contrary to Foucault, the psyche of the subject resists normalization because it "is repeatedly produced.": "[i]t is precisely the possibility of a repetition which . . . proliferates effects which undermine the force of normalization" (93).

3. 50–51; see also Rosemary Hennessey, who complains that, when Butler uses concepts such as "ideology" and "hegemony," "the systemic connections among ideology, state, and labor in the historical materialist theories of Althusser and Gramsci are dropped out" (152).

4. *Bodies* 212–18; she also says that *Bodies that matter* "will pursue the possibility of such disruption but proceed . . . to interrogate the erasures and exclusions that" reveal the limits of constructivism (12).

5. For example, Amy Allen says, "On the one hand, if we are always subjects in the sense of being subjected to myriad power relations, then what seems to be implied is a rather deterministic account of human action that denies the possibility of human agency; on the other hand, if we are always subjects in the sense of having the capacity to act, then the implication seems to be a rather voluntaristic account of human action that denies the grip that power relations have on us" (55).

6. As Butler says, "I whole heartedly agree with Laclau's account of Gramsci" (*Contingencies* 163). In the early *Gender Trouble* she favors an antifoundationalist view of democratic coalition politics because it defers totality and keeps identities open (15–16).

7. 216. Similarly, Moi objects that Butler's identity politics implies that "if we think of the self as coherent, stable, or in anyway unified, we will fall back into the bad picture of sex, and therefore somehow become unable to resist racism and capitalism. Politically speaking, these are puzzling claims, since the whole liberal tradition and indeed the Marxist humanist tradition . . . were quite capable of fighting racism, sexism, and capitalism before poststructuralism came along" (56–57). See also Alan Schrift, who objects that for Butler's purposes the nondeterminist version of classical Marxism, which assumes that class position explains the contrary interests of the ruling elites and oppositional groups, would be better than this Althusserian indeterminacy because the classical Marxism promotes resistance more effectively (16–17, 20).

8. *Ticklish* 217. Similarly, in *Did Somebody Say Totalitarianism?* Žižek complains that those who abandon traditional notions of class struggle accept "the defeat of the Left" as well as the "basic coordinates of liberal democracy," with its attendant multicultural relativism (3; see also Jameson, "Existing" 21, and Foley, "Marxism").

Chapter 5. From Althusserian Science to Foucauldian Materialism

1. For example, in *The Consequences of Pragmatism* Rorty complains that the epistemological norms of traditional philosophy seek but fail to escape the philosopher's determinate historical context or "vocabularies" and to grasp certain, objective truth. He rightly suggests that, if philosophers would recognize their limited historical context, they would not seek an irrefutable argument or defend the scientific method; they would redescribe the vocabularies of others. Philosophy would merge with literary criticism, which is devoted, he says, to such redescription.

2. See, for example, Nancy Hartsock, "Althusser" 34, and Paul Reynolds 268–70. See also Montag, who says that "Jameson found the source of the typically postmodern obsession with disorder and instability to be none other than Pierre Macherey: Macherey's work . . . had become, for Jameson, a symptom of postmodern irrationalism" (Althusser 11).

3. *Consequences* 207. See also *Contingency, Irony, and Solidarity* (1991), where Rorty argues that Jacques Derrida and Michel

Foucault do not make propositional kinds of argument; they critique our vocabularies, denying that any vocabulary and, hence, any rules or conventions are final. He considers these critiques strong forms of irony, but he insists that this "ironizing" does not escape the theorist's private subjectivity. In his terms, "Ironist theorists like Hegel, Nietzsche, Derrida, and Foucault seem to me invaluable in our attempt to form a private self-image, but pretty much useless when it comes to politics" (*Contingency* 83). Moreover, since he identifies literary criticism with this "ironizing," he claims that criticism too is "largely irrelevant to public life" (*Contingency* 83).

Chapter 6. Post-Marxism and Cultural Studies

1. Other historians, including the New Historians, sought more complex, textual, or discursive accounts of a writer's style or era. For instance, like Lukács, Lionel Trilling expected great art to produce an objective insight into the author's sociopolitical context, but he formulated this insight as a matter of the artist's stylistic authenticity and not of society's historical development. See, for example, *The Liberal Imagination*.

2.In *Foucault and Literature*, Simon During also suggests that, because a canonical text such as *Hamlet* "presents an extraordinarily wide range of modes of identity-construction, it can be read as belonging to a range of discursive and socio-political formations" (217). During goes on to argue, however, that traditional textual criticism of Shakespeare escapes these "formations" and keeps the dead author alive and present (221–22).

Works Cited

Adorno, Theodor, and Max Horkheimer. *Dialectic of Enlightenment*. Trans. John Cumming. New York: Continuum Press, 1972.

Allen, Amy. *The power of feminist theory: domination, resistance, solidarity*. Boulder: Westview Press, 1999.

Althusser, Louis. *L'avenir dure longtemps suivi de les faits*. Paris: Éditions STOCK/IMEC, 1992.

———. *Essays in Self-Criticism*. London: New Left Books, 1976.

———. *The Future Lasts Forever*. Ed. Olivier Corpet and Yan Moulier Boutang. Trans. Richard Veasey. New York: The New Press, 1993.

———. *For Marx*. Trans. Ben Brewster. New York: Random House, 1969.

———. *Lenin and Philosophy*. Trans. Ben Brewster. London: Monthly Review Press, 1971.

———. *Positions*. Paris: Éditions Sociales, 1976.

———. *Pour Marx*. Paris: François Maspero, 1977.

Althusser, Louis, and Étienne Balibar. *Reading Capital*. Trans. Ben Brewster. London: New Left Books, 1970.

Altick, Richard D. *The English Common Reader: A Social History of the Mass Reading Public, 1800–1900*. Chicago: U of Chicago P, 1957.

Anderson, Perry. *Arguments within English Marxism*. London: Verso, 1980.

———. *In the Tracks of Historical Materialism*. London: Verso, 1983.

Aronowitz, Stanley. *Science as Power: Discourse and Ideology in Modern Society*. Minneapolis: U of Minnesota P, 1988.

Auerbach, Erich. *Literary Language and Its Public in Late Latin Antiquity and in the Middle Ages*. Trans. Ralph Manheim. Princeton: Princeton UP, 1993.

Austin, John. *How to Do Things with Words*. 2nd Ed. Ed. J. O. Urmson and Marina Sbisà. Cambridge: Harvard UP, 1975.

Awkward, Michael, ed. *New Essays on* Their Eyes Were Watching GOD. Cambridge: Cambridge UP, 1990.

Badiou, Alain. *Ethics: An Essay on the Understanding of Evil*. Trans. and Intro. Peter Hallward. New York: Verso, 2002.

Baldick, Chris. *The Social Mission of English Criticism 1848–1932*. Oxford: Clarendon Press, 1983.

Balibar, Étienne. "Althusser's Object." *Social Text* 39 (Summer 1994): 157–88.

————. *Écrits pour Althusser*. Paris: Éditions La Découverte, 1991.

————. "'The History of Truth': Alain Badiou in French Philosophy." *Radical Philosophy* 115 (September/October 2002): 16–28.

————. "Structural Causality, Overdetermination, and Antagonism." *Postmodern Materialism and the Future of Marxist Theory: Essays in the Althusserian Tradition*. Ed. A. Callari and D. F. Ruccio. Hanover: Wesleyan UP, 1996.

Balibar, Étienne, and Pierre Macherey. "Literature as an Ideological Form: Some Marxist Propositions." *Praxis* 5 (1981): 43–58.

Balibar, Étienne, and Immanuel Wallerstein. *Race, nation, classe Les identités ambiguës*. Paris: Éditions La Décoverte & Syros, 1988.

Barker, Jason. *Alain Badiou: A Critical Introduction*. London: Pluto Press, 2002.

Barrett, Michéle. *The Politics of Truth: From Marx to Foucault*. Stanford: Stanford UP, 1991.

Barthes, Roland. "Science versus Literature." *The Times Literary Supplement*, 28 September 1967, 897–98.

Bell, Daniel. "The End of Ideology in the West." *The End of Ideology Debate*. Ed. Chaim I. Waxman. New York: Funk and Wagnalls, 1968.

Belsey, Catherine. *Critical Practice*. London: Methuen, 1980.

————. "Constructing the Subject: deconstructing the text." *Feminist Criticism and Social Change*. Ed. Judith Lowder Newton and Deborah Rosenfelt. New York: Methuen, 1985. 45–63.

Benhabib, Seyla. "Subjectivity, Historiography, and Politics." *Feminist Contentions: A Philosophical Exchange*, by Judith Butler and others. New York: Routledge, 1995. 107–25.

Bennett, Tony. *Bond and Beyond: The Political Career of a Hero*. New York: Methuen, 1987.

————. *Culture: A Reformer's Science*. St. Leonards, Australia: Allyn and Unwin, 1998.

———. *Formalism and Marxism*. London: Methuen and Co., 1979.

———. *Outside Literature*. New York: Routledge, 1990.

———. "Texts in History: The Determinations of Readings and Their Texts." *The Journal of the MMLA* 18 (Fall 1985): 1–16.

Benton, Ted. *The Rise and Fall of Structural Marxism*. London: MacMillan, 1984.

Berman, Russell. *Modern Culture and Critical Theory: Art, Politics, and the Legacy of the Frankfurt School*. Madison: The U of Wisconsin P, 1989.

Bernal, Martin. *Black Athena: The Afroasiatic Roots of Classical Civilization*. New Brunswick: Rutgers UP, 1987. Vol 1.

Bernstein, J. M. *The Philosophy of the Novel: Lukács, Marxism, and the Dialectics of Form*. Minneapolis: U of Minnesota P, 1984.

Best, Steven, and Douglas Kellner. *Postmodern Theory: Critical Interrogations*. New York: The Guilford Press, 1991.

Bové, Paul. *In the Wake of THEORY*. Hanover: Wesleyan UP, 1992.

———. *Mastering Discourse: The Politics of Intellectual Culture*. Durham: Duke UP, 1992.

Brantlinger, Patrick. *Crusoe's Footprints: Cultural Studies in Britain and America*. New York: Routledge, 1990.

Brenkman, John. *Culture and Domination*. Ithaca: Cornell UP, 1987.

Brzezinski, Zbigniew, and Carl J. Friedrich. *Totalitarian Dictatorship and Autocracy*. Cambridge: Harvard UP, 1956.

Butler, Judith. *Bodies That Matter: On the Discursive Limits of "Sex."* New York: Routledge, 1993.

———. "Contingent Foundations." *Feminist Contentions: A Philosophical Exchange*, by Judith Butler and others. New York: Routledge, 1995. 35–57.

———. *Excitable Speech: A Politics of the Performative*. New York: Routledge, 1997.

———. *Gender Trouble: Feminism and the Subversion of Identity*. New York: Routledge, 1990.

———. "Poststructuralism and PostMarxism." *diacritics: a review of contemporary criticism* 23:4 (Winter 1993): 3–11.

———. *The Psychic Life of Power*. Stanford: Stanford UP, 1997.

———. "Sexual Inversions." *Foucault and the Critique of Institutions*. Ed. John Caputo and Mark Yount. University Park: Pennsylvania State UP, 1993.

Butler, Judith, Ernesto Laclau, and Slavoj i ek. *Contingency, Hegemony, Universality: Contemporary Dialogues on the Left*. London: Verso, 2000.

Callari, Anthony, and David F. Ruccio. "Introduction." *Postmodern Materialism and the Future of Marxist Theory: Essays in the Althusserian Tradition*. Ed. Anthony Callari and David F. Ruccio. Hanover: Wesleyan UP, 1996: 1–48.

Callinicos, Alex. *The Revenge of History: Marxism and the East European Revolutions*. Oxford: Polity Press, 1991.

———. "What Is Living and What Is Dead in the Philosophy of Althusser." *The Althusserian Legacy*. Ed. E. Ann Kaplan and Michael Sprinker. New York: Verso, 1993. 39–49.

Canguilem, Georges. *The normal and the pathological*. Boston: D. Reidel , 1978.

Caputo, John, and Mark Yount, eds. *Foucault and the Critique of Institutions*. University Park: Pennsylvania State UP, 1993.

Carver, Terrell. *The Postmodern Marx*. University Park: Pennsylvania State UP, 1998.

Caute, David. *The Illusion: An Essay on Politics, Theatre, and the Novel*. London: Andre Deutsch Limited, 1971.

Cohen, Stephen F. *Rethinking the Soviet Experience: Politics and History since 1917*. New York: Oxford UP, 1985.

Conley, Thomas M. *Rhetoric in the European Tradition*. Urbana-Champaign: U of Illinois P, 1990.

Critchley, Simon. "Ethics, Politics and Radical Democracy—the History of a Disagreement." *CULTURE MACHINE* 4 (2002) <http://culturemachine.tees.ac.uk/frm_fl.htm>.

Cullenberg, Stephen. "Althusser and the Decentering of the Marxist Totality." *Postmodern Materialism and the Future of Marxist Theory: Essays in the Althusserian Tradition*. Ed. Anthony Callari and David F. Ruccio. Hanover: Wesleyan UP, 1996: 120–49.

Daniels, Robert V. *The End of the Communist Revolution*. London: Routledge, 1993.

Davies, Tony. *Humanism*. London: Routledge, 1997.

Davis, Angela Y. "Women and Capitalism: Dialectics of Oppression and Liberation." *The Black Feminist Reader*. Ed. Joy James and T. Denean Sharpley-Whiting. Oxford: Blackwell, 2000. 146–82.

De Beauvoir, Simone. *The Second Sex*. Trans. and Ed. H. M. Parshley. New York: Vintage Books, 1989.

Deleuze, Gilles. *Foucault*. Paris: Les Éditions de Minuit, 1986.

Derrida, Jacques. "Marx's Purloined Letter." *New Left Review* 209 (January/February 1995): 75–108.

———. "Signature, Event, Context." *Glyph* 1 (1977): 172–97.

———. *Specters of Marx: The State of the Debt, the Work of Mourning, and the New International.* Intro. Bernd Magnus and Stephen Cullenberg. Trans. Peggy Kamuf. New York: Routledge, 1994.

———. *Spectres de Marx: L'État de la dette, le travail du deuil et la nouvelle Internationale.* Paris: Éditions Galilée, 1993.

Doyle, Brian. *English and Englishness.* London: Routledge, 1989.

Dreyfus, Hubert L., and Paul Rabinow. *Michel Foucault: Beyond Structuralism and Hermeneutics.* 2nd Ed. Chicago: U of Chicago P, 1983.

During, Simon. *Foucault and Literature: Towards a Genealogy of Writing.* London and New York: Routledge, 1992.

Dworkin, Dennis. *Cultural Marxism in Postwar Britain: History, the New Left, and the Origins of Cultural Studies.* Durham: Duke UP, 1997.

Eagleton, Terry. *Criticism and Ideology.* London: Verso Books, 1978.

———. *The Ideology of the Aesthetic.* Cambridge MA: Basil Blackwell, 1990.

———. *Marxism and Literary Criticism.* Berkeley: U of California P, 1976.

———. "The Revolt of the Reader." *New Literary History* 13 (1982): 449–52.

Easthope, Anthony. *British Post-structuralism since 1968.* London: Routledge, 1988.

Easthope, Anthony, and Kate McGowan, eds. *A Critical and Cultural Theory Reader.* Toronto: U of Toronto P, 1992.

Ebenstein, William, and Edwin Fogelman. *Today's Isms: Communism, Fascism, Capitalism, Socialism.* 9th ed. Englewood Cliffs: Prentice-Hall, 1985.

Elliot, Gregory. *Althusser: The Detour of Theory.* London: Verso, 1987.

———, ed. *Althusser: A Critical Reader.* Cambridge: Blackwell, 1994.

Ellis, John M. *Literature Lost: Social Agendas and the Corruption of the Humanites.* New Haven: Yale UP, 1997.

Fleming, Marie. *Emancipation and Illusion: Rationality and Gender in Habermas' Theory of Modernity.* University Park: Pennsylvania State UP, 1997.

Flynn, Thomas. *Sartre, Foucault, and Historical Reason*. Chicago: U of Chicago P, 1997.

Foley, Barbara. "Marxism in the Poststructuralist Moment: Some Notes on the Problem of Revising Marx." *Cultural Critique* 15 (Spring 1990): 5–37.

Foucault, Michel. *The Archaeology of Knowledge*. Trans. A. M. Sheridan Smith. New York: Harper and Row, 1976.

———. *Discipline and Punish: The Birth of the Prison*. Trans. Alan Sheridan. New York: Vintage/Random House, 1979.

———. *Histoire de la folie à l'âge classique*. Paris: Éditions Gallimard, 1972.

———. *Histoire de la sexualité: La Volonté de savoir*. Paris: Éditions Gallimard, 1976.

———. *Les mots et les choses: une archéologie des sciences humaines*. Paris: Éditions Gallimard, 1966.

———. *Madness and Civilization: A History of Insanity in the Age of Reason*. Trans. R. Howard. New York: Vintage/Random House, 1973.

———. *The Order of Things: An Archaeology of the Human Sciences*. Trans. Alan Sheridan. New York: Pantheon Press, 1970.

———. *Power / Knowledge: Selected Interviews and Other Writings 1972–1977*. Ed. Colin Gordon. Trans. Colin Gordon and others. New York: Pantheon Books. 1980.

———. "Qu'est-ce que les Lumières?" *Dits et Écrits 1954–1988*. Ed. Daniel Defert, François Ewald, and Jacques Lagrange. Paris: Éditions Gallimard, 1994. IV, 562–78.

———. *Surveiller et punir: Naissance de la prison*. Paris: Éditions Gallimard, 1975.

Fougeyrollas, Pierre. *Contre Lévi-Strauss, Lacan, et Althusser: Trois essais sur l'obscurantisme contemporain*. Savelli: Éditions librairie de la Jonquière, 1976.

Freedman, Carl. "The Interventional Marxism of Louis Althusser." *Rethinking Marxism* 3: 3–4 (Fall-Winter 1990): 309–28.

Frijhoff, Willem. "Foucault Reformed by Certeau: Historical Strategies of Discipline and Everyday Tactics of Appropriation." *Cultural History After Foucault*. Ed. John Neubauer. New York: Aldine de Gruyter, 1999. 83–100.

Fromm, Eric. *Marx's Concept of Man*. New York: Frederick Unger, 1961.

Frow, John, *Marxism and Literary History*. Cambridge: Harvard UP, 1986.

——. *Cultural Studies and Cultural Value*. Oxford: Clarendon Press, 1995.

——. "Cultural Studies and the Neoliberal Imagination." *The Yale Journal of Criticism* 12:2 (1999): 423–430.

Gates, Henry Louis, Jr. "Afterward." *Their Eyes Were Watching God*. New York: Harper and Row, 1990.

Gearhart, Suzanne. "The Taming of Michel Foucault: New Historicism, Psychoanalysis, and the Subversion of Power." *New Literary History* 28 (1997): 457–80.

Giroux, Henry. *Theory and Resistance in Education: A Pedagogy for the Opposition*. South Hadley, MA: Bergin and Garvey, 1983.

Glucksmann, André. "A Ventriloquist Marxism." *Western Marxism: A Critical Reader*. Ed. *New Left Review*. London: Verso, 1977. 273–314.

——. *The Master Thinkers*. Trans. Brian Pearce. New York: Harper and Row, 1980.

Goldstein, Philip. *The Politics of Literary Criticism: An Introduction to Marxist Cultural Theory*. Gainesville: The U of Florida P, 1990.

Graff, Gerald. "Co-optation." *The New Historicism*. Ed. H. Aram Veeser. New York: Routledge, 1989. 169–173.

——. *Professing Literature: An Institutional History*. Chicago: U of Chicago P, 1987.

Grafton, Anthony, and Lisa Jardine. *From Humanism to the Humanities: Education and the Liberal Arts in Fifteenth and Sixteenth-Century Europe*. Cambridge: Harvard UP, 1986.

Guillory, John. *Cultural Capital: The Problem of Literary Canon Formation*. Chicago: The U of Chicago P, 1993.

Gutting, Gary. "Foucault and the History of Madness." *The Cambridge Companion to Foucault*. Ed.Gary Gutting. Cambridge: Cambridge UP, 1994. 47–70.

Habermas, Jürgen. *Knowledge and Human Interests*. Trans. Jeremy J. Shapiro. Boston: Beacon Press, 1971.

——. *The Philosophical Discourse of Modernity*. Trans. Frederick Lawrence. Cambridge: The MIT Press, 1987.

Han, Béatrice. *L'ontologie manquée de Michel Foucault entre l'historique et le transcendental*. Grenoble: Éditions Jérôme Millon: 1998.

Hardt, Michael, and Antonio Negri. *Empire*. Cambridge: Harvard UP, 2000.

Harland, Richard. *Superstructuralism: the philosophy of structuralism and post-structuralism*. London: Methuen, 1987.

Hartsock, Nancy C. M. "Louis Althusser's Structuralist Marxism: Political Clarity and Theoretical Distortions." *Rethinking Marxism* 4:4 (Winter 1991): 10–40.

———. "Postmodernism and Political Change: Issues for Feminist Theory." *Cultural Critique* 14 (Winter 1989–1990): 3–15.

Hazlett, Moyra. *Marxist Literary and Cultural Theories.* New York: St. Martin's Press, 2000.

Hegel, G. W. F. *The Phenomenology of Mind.* 2nd ed. Trans. and Intro. J. B. Baillie. New York: MacMillan, 1949.

Hennessy, Rosemary. "Queer Visibility in Commodity Culture." *Social Postmodernism: Beyond Identity Politics.* Ed. Linda Nicholson and Steven Seidman. Cambridge: Cambridge UP, 1995. 142–83.

Hirsch, E. D., Jr. *The Aims of Interpretation.* Chicago: U of Chicago P, 1976.

Hirst, Paul. *On Law and Ideology.* Atlantic Highlands NJ: Humanities Press, 1979.

———. *Marxism and Historical Writing.* London: Routledge and Kegan Paul, 1985.

Ingram, David. "Foucault and Habermas on the Subject of Reason." *The Cambridge Companion to Foucault.* Ed. Gary Gutting. Cambridge: Cambridge UP, 1994. 215–61.

Jameson, Fredric. "Actually Existing Marxism." *Marxism Beyond Marxism.* Ed. Saree Makdisi, Cesare Casarino, and Rebecca Karl. New York: Routledge, 1996. 14–54.

———. *Fables of Aggression: Wyndham Lewis, the Modernist as Fascist.* Los Angeles: U of California P, 1979.

———. *Marxism and Form: Twentieth-Century Dialectical Theories of Literature.* Princeton: Princeton UP, 1971.

———. "On 'Cultural Studies.'" *Social Text* 34: 17–52.

———. *The Political Unconscious: Narrative as a Socially Symbolic Act.* Ithaca: Cornell UP, 1981.

———. "Postmodernism, or The Cultural Logic of Late Capitalism." *New Left Review* 146 (July–August 1984): 53–92.

———. *The Prison-House of Language.* Princeton: Princeton UP, 1972.

———. "Regarding Postmodernism—A Conversation with Fredric Jameson." *Social Text* 17: 29–54.

Jay, Martin. *Marxism and Totality: The Adventures of a Concept from Lukács to Habermas* Berkeley: U of California P, 1984.

Kamps, Ivo. "Introduction." *Materialist Shakespeare: A History.* Ed. Ivo Kamps. London: Verso, 1995. 1–19.

Kamuf, Peggy. *The Division of Literature: Or The University in Deconstruction*. Chicago: The U of Chicago P, 1997.

Kellner, Douglas. "the obsolescence of marxism?" In *whither marxism? global crises in international perspective*. Ed. Bernd Magnus and Stephen Cullenberg. New York: Routledge, 1995. 3–30.

Kitching, Gavin. *Marxism and Science: Analysis of an Obsession*. University Park: Pennsylvania State UP, 1994.

Kögler, Hans Herbert. *The Power of Dialogue: Critical Hermeneutics after Gadamer and Foucault*. Trans. Paul Hendrickson. Cambridge: MIT Press, 1996.

Krancberg, Sigmund. *A Soviet Postmortem: Philosophical Roots of the "Grand Failure."* Boston: Rowman and Littlefield, 1994.

Kurzweil, Edith. "Althusser's Madness: Theory or Practice?" *Partisan Review* LXI:3 (1994): 514–17.

La Capra, Dominick. *Soundings in Critical Theory*. Ithaca: Cornell UP, 1989.

Laclau, Ernesto. *Emancipation(s)*. London: Verso, 1996.

———. *New Reflections on the Revolution of Our Time*. London: Verso, 1993.

———. "'The Time Is Out of Joint'." *Diacritics* 25:2 (Summer 1995): 86–97.

Laclau, Ernesto, and Chantal Mouffe. *Hegemony and Socialist Strategy*. London: Verso, 1985.

Larrain, Jorge. *Ideology and Cultural Identity: Modernity and the Third World Presence*. Cambridge, UK: Polity Press, 1994.

Latimer, Dan. *Contemporary Critical Theory*. New York: Harcourt, Brace, Jovanovich, 1989.

Le Court, Dominique. *Marxism and Epistemology*. Atlantic Highlands, NJ: Humanities Press, 1969.

Lemert, Charles C., and Garth Gillan. *Michel Foucault: Social Theory and Transgression*. New York: Columbia UP, 1982.

Lewin, Moshe. *The Gorbachev Phenomenon: A Historical Phenomenon*. Berkeley: U of California P, 1988.

———. *The Making of the Soviet System: Essays in the Social History of Interwar Russia*. New York: Pantheon Books, 1985.

Looser, Devoney. "Feminist Theory and Foucault: A Bibliographic Essay." *Style* 26 (Winter 1992): 593–603.

Lukács, Georg. *History and Class Consciousness: Studies in Marxist Dialectics*. Trans. Rodney Livingstone. Cambridge: The MIT Press, 1971.

——. *The Theory of the Novel: A Historico-Philosophical Essay on the Forms of Great Epic Literature*. Trans. Anna Bostock. Cambridge: The MIT Press, 1971.

Lyotard, Jean-François. "La Place de l'alienation dans le retournement Marxiste." *A la Derive a Partir de Marx et Freud*. Paris: Union Generales d'Éditions, 1973. 78–166.

——. *The Postmodern Condition: A Report on Knowledge*. Trans. Geoff Bennington and Brian Massumi. Minneapolis: U of Minnesota P, 1984.

MacDowell, Diane, *Theories of Discourse: An Introduction*. Oxford: Basil Blackwell, 1986.

Macherey, Pierre. *A quoi pense la littérature? Exercices de philosophie littéraire*. Paris: UPes of France, 1990.

——. *Hegel ou Spinoza*. Paris: Maspero, 1979. Paris: University Presses of France, 1999.

——. *Histoires de dinosaure Faire de la Philosophie 1965–1997*.

——. "In a materialist way." *Philosophy in France Today*. Ed. Alan Montefiore. Cambridge: Cambridge UP, 1983.

——. *In a Materialist Way Selected Essays by Pierre Macherey*. Ed. Warren Montag. Trans. Ted Stolze. London: Verso, 1998.

——. *The Object of Literature*. Trans. David Macey. Cambridge: Cambridge UP, 1995.

——. *A Theory of Literary Production*. Trans. Geoffrey Wall. London: Routledge and Kegan Paul, 1978.

——. *The Object of Literature*. Trans. David Macey. Cambridge: Cambridge UP, 1995.

Marcuse, Herbert. *One-Dimensional Man*. Boston: Beacon Press, 1964.

Marsden, Richard. *The Nature of Capital: Marx after Foucault*. London; Routlege, 1999.

Martin, Randy. *On Your Marx: Rethinking Socialism and the Left*. Minneapolis: U of Minnesota P, 2002.

Marty, Éric. *Louis Althusser, un sujet sans process Anatomie d'un passé très recent*. Paris: Éditions Gallimard, 1999.

Marx, Karl. *Capital*. Moscow: Progress Publishers, 1965.

Marx, Karl, and Friedrich Engels. *The German Ideology*. Ed. R. Pascal. New York: International Publishers, 1947.

McClellan, David. *Ideology*. Minneapolis: U of Minnesota P, 1986.

McNay, Lois. *Foucault and Feminism*. Cambridge: Polity Press, 1992. Boston: Northeastern UP, 1993.

McWhorter, Ladelle. *Bodies and Pleasures: Foucault and the Politics of Sexual Normalization*. Bloomington: Indiana UP, 1999.

Meek, Ronald L. *Smith, Marx, and After: Ten Essays in the Development of Economic Thought*. New York: Wiley, 1977.

Megill, Alan. *Prophets of Extremity: Nietzsche, Heidegger, Foucault, Derrida*. Berkeley: U of California P, 1985.

Meyer, Alfred. G. *Communism*. 3rd edition. New York: Random House, 1967.

Miklitsch, Robert. "The Rhetoric of Post-Marxism: Discourse and Institutionality in Laclau and Mouffe, Resnick and Wolff." *Social Text* 45: 167–96.

Middleton, Sue. *Disciplining Sexuality: Foucault, Life Histories, and Education*. New York: Teachers College Press, 1998.

Miller, Toby. *Technologies of Truth: Cultural Citizenship and the Popular Media*. Minneapolis: U of Minnesota P, 1998.

———. *The Well-Tempered Self: Citizenship, Culture, and the Postmodern Subject*. Baltimore: Johns Hopkins UP, 1993.

Moi, Toril. *What is a Woman? and Other Essays*. Oxford: Oxford UP, 1999.

Montag, Warren. "Introduction." *In a Materialist Way: Selected Essays by Pierre Macherey*. Ed. Warren Montag. Trans. Ted Stolze. London: Verso, 1998. 3–14.

———. *Louis Althusser*. New York: Palgrave MacMillan, 2003.

———. "Marxism and Psychoanalysis: The Impossible Encounter." *The Minnesota Review* XXIII (Fall 1984): 70–85.

———. "What Is at Stake in the Debate on Postmodernism?" *Postmodernism and Its Discontents: Theories, Practices*. Ed. E. Ann Kaplan. New York: Verso, 1988. 88–103.

Morris, Meagan. "The Pirate's Fiancée: Feminists and Philosophers, or Maybe Tonight It'll Happen." *Feminism and Foucault: Reflections on Resistance*. Ed. Irene Diamond and Lee Quinby. Boston: Northeastern UP, 1988: 21–42.

Munck, Ronaldo. *Marx @ 2000: Late Marxist Perspectives*. London: ZED Books, 2000.

Mustapha, Abdul-Karim, and Bülent Eken. "Introduction: Communism in the Grand Style." *Rethinking Marxism* 13:4/5: 1–7.

Nelson, Kai. "The Concept of Ideology: Some Marxist and Non-Marxist Conceptualizations." *Rethinking Marxism* 2:4 (Winter 1989): 146–73.

Newman, Gerald. *The Rise of English Nationalism: A Cultural History, 1740–1830*. New York: St. Martin's Press, 1987.

Nussbaum, Martha. "The Professor of Parody: The Hip Defeatism of Judith Butler." *The New Republic*, February 22, 1999, 37.

O'Hara, Daniel. T. "What Was Foucault?" *After Foucault: Humanistic Knowledge, Postmodern Challenges*. Ed. Jonathan Arac. New Brunswick: Rutgers UP, 1988.

Olssen, Mark. *Michel Foucault: Materialism and Education*. Westport: Bergin and Garvey, 1999.

Ong, Walter. J. *Rhetoric, Romance, and Technology: Studies in the Interaction of Expression and Culture*. Ithaca: Cornell UP, 1971.

Ozinga, J. R. *Communism: The Story of the Idea and Its Implementation*. 2nd Ed. Englewood Cliffs NJ: Prentice-Hall, 1991.

Parker, Andrew. "Futures for Marxism: An Appreciation of Althusser," *Diacritics* 15:4 (Winter 1985): 57–93.

Parrinder, Patrick. *Authors and Authority: A Study of English Literary Criticism and its Relation to Culture, 1750–1900*. London: Routledge and Kegan Paul, 1977.

Pietz, William. "The Post-Colonialism of Cold War Discourse." *Social Text* 19/20 (Fall 1988): 56–76.

Porter, Carolyn. "Are We Being Historical Yet?" *Southern Atlantic Quarterly* 87:4 (Fall 1988): 743–86.

Poster, Mark. *Foucault, Marxism, and History: Mode of Production versus Mode of Information*. Cambridge: Polity Press, 1984.

Poulantzas, Nicos. *L'Etat, le Pouvoir, le Socialisme*. Paris: Presses Universitaires de France, 1978.

Prado, C. G. *Starting with Foucault: An Introduction to Genealogy*. Boulder: Westview Press, 1995.

Rajchman, John. "Foucault's Dilemma." *Social Text* 8 (Winter 1983/84): 1–21.

Ramazanoglu, Caroline, ed. *Up Against Foucault: Explorations of Some Tensions between Foucault and Feminism*. London and New York: Routledge, 1993.

Rancière, Jacques. *La leçon d'Althusser*. Paris: Gallimard, 1974.

———. "La Scène du texte." *Politique et philosophie dans l'œuvre de Louis Althusser*. Ed. Sylvain Lazarus. Paris: Presses Universitaires de France, 1993. 47–67.

Resch, Robert Paul. *Althusser and the Renewal of Marxist Social Theory*. Berkeley: U of California P, 1992.

———. "Modernism, Postmodernism, and Social Theory: A Comparison of Althusser and Foucault." *Poetics Today* 10:3 (Fall 1989): 511–49.

Resnick, Stephen A., and Richard D Wolff. "Althusser's Liberation of Marxist Theory." *The Althusserian Legacy*. Ed. E. Ann Kaplan and Michael Sprinker. New York: Verso, 1993. 59–72.

———. *Class Theory and History: Capitalism and Communism in the U.S.S.R.* New York: Routledge, 2002.

———. *Knowledge and Class: A Marxian Critique of Political Economy* Chicago: The U of Chicago P, 1987.

———. "State Capitalism in the USSR? A High-Stakes Debate." *Rethinking Marxism* 6:2 (Summer 1993): 46–68.

Reynolds, Paul. "Post-Marxism: Radical Political Theory and Practice Beyond Marxism?" *Marxism, the Millennium and Beyond*. Ed. Mark Cowling and Paul Reynolds. New York: Palgrave, 2000.

Robbins, Bruce. *Secular Vocations: Intellectuals, Professionalism, Culture*. New York: Verso. 1993.

Rorty, Richard. *Consequences of Pragmatism (Essays: 1972–1980)*. Minneapolis: U of Minnesota P, 1982.

———. *Contingency, Irony, Solidarity*. Cambridge: Cambridge UP, 1989.

———. "Moral Identity and Private Autonomy: The Case of Foucault." *Essays on Heidegger and Others*. Cambridge: Cambridge UP, 1991. 193–98.

Rothenberg, Molly Anne, and Joseph Valente. "Performative Chic: The Fantasy of a Performative Politics." *College Literature* 24:1 (Fall 1997): 295–304.

Ryan, Michael. "The Empire of Wealth." *Politics and Culture* 1, 2001. 7 Jan. 2002 <http://laurel.conncoll.edu/politicsandculture>.

Said, Edward. *The World, the Text, and the Critic*. Cambridge: Harvard UP, 1983.

Sandford, Stella. "Sex, Gender, and 'Woman' in Simone de Beauvoir and Judith Butler." *Radical Philosophy* 97 (September/October 1999): 18–29.

San Juan, E., Jr. *Hegemony and Strategies of Transgression: Essays in Cultural Studies and Comparative Literature*. Albany: State U of New York P, 1995.

Sawicki, Jana. *Disciplining Foucault: Feminism, Power, and the Body*. New York: Routledge, 1991.

———. "Identity Politics and Sexual Freedom: Foucault and Feminism." *Michel Foucault: Critical Assessments*. Ed. Barry Smart. London: Routledge, 1995. VI, 353–65.

Sheridan, Alan. *The Will to Truth*. New York: Methuen, 1980.

Shrift, Alan D. "Judith Butler: Une Nouvelle Existentialiste?" *Philosophy Today* 12 (Spring 2001): 12–23.

Sim, Stuart. *Post-Marxism: An Intellectual History*. New York: Routledge, 2000.

Simons, Jonathan. *Foucault and the Political*. London: Routledge, 1994.

Smart, Barry. *Foucault, Marxism, and Critique*. London: Routledge and Kegan Paul, 1983.

———. "On the Subjects of Sexuality, Ethics, and Politics in the Work of Foucault." *boundary 2* 18:1 (Spring 1991): 201–25.

———. "The Politics of Truth and the Problem of Hegemony." *Foucault: A Critical Reader*. Ed. David Couzens Hoy. Oxford: Basil Blackwell, 1986. 157–74.

———, ed. *Michel Foucault I. Critical Assessments: Archaeology, Genealogy, and Politics*. London and New York: Routledge, 1994.

Smith, Anna Marie. *Laclau and Mouffe: The Radical Democratic Imaginary*. London: Routledge, 1998.

Smith, Barbara Herrnstein. *Contingencies of Value: Alternative Perspectives of Critical Theory*. Cambridge: Harvard UP, 1988.

Smith, Erin A. *Hard-Boiled: Working-Class Readers and Pulp Magazines*. Philadelpha: Temple UP, 2000.

Smith, Paul. *Discerning the Subject*. Minneapolis: U of Minnesota P, 1988.

Smith, Stephen B. "Ideology and Interpretation: The Case of Althusser." *Poetics Today* 10:3 (Fall 1989): 493–509.

———. *Reading Althusser: An Essay on Structural Marxism*. Ithaca: Cornell UP, 1984.

Spivak, Gayatri. *The Spivak Reader: Selected Works of Gayatri Chakravorty Spivak*. Ed. Donna Landry and Gerald MacLean. New York: Routledge, 1996.

Sprinker, Michael. "The Current Conjuncture in Theory." *College English* 51:8 (December 1989), 825–34.

———. *Imaginary Relations: Aesthetics and Ideology in the Theory of Historical Materialism*. New York: Verso, 1987.

———. "The War Against Theory." *The Minnesota Review* 39 (Fall/Winter 1992/93): 103–21.

Sprinker, Michael, and E. Ann Kaplan, Ann, eds. *The Althusserian Legacy*. New York: Verso, 1993.

Steiner, George. "Stranglehold." *The New Yorker*, February 21, 1994, 114–18.

Strong, Tracy B., and Frank Andreas Sposito. "Habermas' Significant Other." *The Cambridge Guide to Habermas*. Ed. Stephen K. White. Cambridge: Cambridge UP, 1995. 263–88.

Swingewood, A. *The Novel and Revolution*. London: MacMillan, 1976.

Thompson, E. P. *The Poverty of Theory and Other Essays*. London: Merlin Press, 1978.

Todd, May. *Between Genealogy and Epistemology: Psychology, Politics, and Knowledge in the Thought of Michel Foucault*. University Park: Penn State UP, 1993.

Torfing, Jacob. *New Theories of Discourse: Laclau, Mouffe, and Zizek*. Oxford: Blackwell, 1999.

Trilling, Lionel. *The Liberal Imagination: Essays on Literature and Society*. Garden City: Doubleday, 1953.

Tucker, Robert C. "Stalinism as Revolution from Above." *Stalinism: Essays in Historical Interpretation*. Ed. Robert C. Tucker. New York: W. W. Norton, 1977. 77–108.

Valdés, Mario. J. "Answering Foucault: Notes on Modes of Order in the Cultural World and the Making of History." *Cultural History After Foucault*. Ed. John Neubauer. New York: Aldine de Gruyter, 1999. 101–120.

Visker, Rudi. *Michel Foucault: Genealogy as Critique*. Trans. Chris Turner. London: Verso, 1995.

Walker, Alice. "A Cautionary Tale and a Partisan View." *Zora Neale Hurston*. Ed. and Intro. Harold Bloom. New York: Chelsea House, 1986. 63–69.

———. "Looking for Zora." *I Love Myself When I am Laughing . . . And Then Again When I am Looking Mean and Impressive: A Zora Neale Hurston Reader*. Ed. Alice Walker. Intro. Mary Helen Washington. New York: The Feminist Press, 1979. 297–313.

Walton, Paul, and Andrew Gamble. *From Alienation to Surplus Value*. London: Sheed and Ward, 1972.

Walton, Priscilla L., and Manina Jones. *Detective Agency: Women Rewriting the Hard-Boiled Tradition*. Los Angeles: U of California P, 1999.

Walzer, Michael. "The Politics of Michel Foucault." *Foucault: A Critical Reader*. Ed. David Couzens Hoy. Oxford: Basil Blackwell, 1986: 51–68.

Washington, Mary Helen. "Foreword." *Their Eyes Were Watching God*. New York: Harper and Row, 1990.

Wellek, René. *A History of Modern Criticism: 1750–1950*. New Haven: Yale UP, 1965. 5 vols.

Wellek, René, and Austin Warren. *Theory of Literature*. New York: Harcourt, Brace, and World, 1956.

Whigham, Frank. *Ambition and Privilege: The Social Tropes of Elizabethan Courtesy Theory*. Berkeley: U of California P, 1984.

Williams, Raymond. *Marxism and Literature*. New York: Oxford UP, 1976.

———. *Culture and Society*. New York: Columbia UP, 1983.

———. *Problems in Materialism and Culture*. London: Verso, 1980.

Žižek, Slavoj. "Beyond Discourse-Analysis." *New Revolutions in Our Time*. Ed. Ernesto Laclau. London: Verso, 1993. 249–60.

———. *Did Somebody Say Totalitarianism? Five Interventions in the (Mis)use of a Notion*. London: Verso, 2001.

———. *The Ticklish Subject: The Absent Center of Political Ontology*. New York: Verso, 1999.

INDEX